THE CALTEX BOOK OF MAORI LORE

THE CALTEX BOOK

A. H. & A. W. REED

Wellington - Sydney - London

OF MAORI LORE

TEXT BY JAMES COWAN

Revised by J. B. Palmer

ILLUSTRATED BY DENNIS TURNER

First edition 1959
Reprinted 1960, 1961, 1962, 1965, 1967, 1969, 1971, 1972 and 1974
A. H. & A. W. REED LTD.
182 Wakefield Street, Wellington
51 Whiting Street, Artarmon, Sydney
11 Southampton Row, London, WC1B SHA
also
29 Dacre Street, Auckland
165 Cashel Street, Christchurch

This book was originally written at the request of the Texas Company (Australasia) Ltd., predecessors in business of Caltex Oil (N.Z.) Ltd. The thanks of the publishers are extended to Caltex for the cooperation which made the book available in this popular edition; and to Lt-Col C. M. Bennett, who advised on the manuscript; and to Mr J. B. Palmer, former editor of *The Journal of the Polynesian Society,* who has revised and edited the work.

ISBN 0 589 00014 4

Printed by Wright & Carman Ltd., Trentham

CONTENTS

JAMES COWAN

THE NAME of James Cowan will probably not be familiar to young readers today. To some of those of an older age group, Cowan was the writer who fired their imagination and warmed their enthusiasm for tales of the bush, the border and the coast of this country.

Never sentimental, but always romantic, James Cowan reflected the spirit of his age, a period when there was a growing interest in the Maori race and a greater hope for its future than in the years that preceded it. As a young journalist, he came to respect the older generation of Maori, whose colourful past made such an impression on him. His knowledge of the language enabled him to gather stories of past incidents from old Maoris who had been actual participants in stirring events, and Cowan found great satisfaction in re-creating the often exciting days of their youth. In doing this, his characters became alive and intimate, full of what Cowan believed to be the spirit of the old-time Maori.

An association of people with landscape is the main feature of Cowan's work. Although there is something to interest the serious student in most of his writing, one remembers best his descriptive passages of persons and places, together with incidents linking both. At times one may detect the influence of his vocation, but his writing was always sincere and sympathetic.

James Cowan was responsible for an upsurge of interest in the Maori race. It is hoped that this edition of an unpublished Cowan manuscript will arouse interest in his other books and in the history and traditions that he sought to preserve.

J. B. PALMER

PREFACE

"IT IS REFRESHING," said an English writer, referring to the Biblical prophets and poets, "to get back to the thoughts of men whose chief library was their mind and whose university was the traditions of their race." This remark might, with like truth, be applied to the Maori people and to a study of the rich store of tradition and poetry embodied in their literature. There is a definite cultural value in the language, philosophy, legend and song of the race, and the national characteristics of the New Zealanders of the future are bound to be influenced appreciably by the Maori.

The strain of Maori blood in the population of the country is widely diffused, and with the spread of education, and the raising of the level of Maori life, the process of racial blending is likely to advance. Interest and pride in the history, the achievements and the peculiar artistic genius of the Maori is, too, likely to assist in the formation of the true New Zealand spirit. Here we have an inexhaustible fount of inspiration which will come to be valued more and more by members of both sections of the Dominion's population. Today, the Maori language, traditions and artcraft, with landscape and forest life, are often drawn upon to give the distinctive New Zealand touch to some great occasion.

The Maori tongue will not perish, or become a purely academic study. It will persist, like the Welsh. The New Zealand education system of the near future, we may hope, will not subordinate the things that are New Zealand to those of other countries, and will give the language the recognition to which it is entitled. The industrial rebirth of the Maori, the example the Maori farmer sets to many of his pakeha neighbours, will be reinforced by an increasing popular concern in all the features of an ancient life which enrich the New Zealand of today, and preserve heroic memories and poetic pictures of the past. These are a pleasing foil to the speed, stress and bustle of the modern world.

In this little book a sketch is given of the past and present of the Maori, the great ocean voyages of the Maori-Polynesian ancestors, the coming to New Zealand and the daily life of the people in this country; religion and sacred lore, the language, and the wealth of poetry and legend. Other characteristics of the Maori in peace and war are discussed in later chapters. In the chapter on warfare, the military genius of the people and their skill in fortification are described, and a fine old chief of the Arawa tribe is sketched as a type of the past generation of warrior.

Other chapters deal with the institution of tapu and related beliefs; the lore of the forest and the bird-hunting practices of the native bushman; artcraft and design, with particular reference to wood-carving and house decoration; the war-canoe of the past and the exciting sport of canoe-racing, which still survives on the Waikato River; and various amusements of the Maori, past and present.

In the chapter on ceremonies for the dead, a description is given of a heart-stirring tribal tangihanga, or mourning gathering, at Matata, on the Bay of Plenty coast.

1

THE MAORI PEOPLE

THE NEW ZEALAND MAORI RACE, one of the most sturdy, independent and progressive branches of the Polynesian family, is numerically the strongest member of that widely distributed people. The Maori and half-caste population of our country shows a steady annual increase; it now stands at between 145,000 and 150,000. This increase has only become manifest during the last quarter of a century, or so. At the beginning of the present century it was customary to regard the Maori as a dying race. This belief has happily been reversed. The increase is in great measure due to the improved hygienic conditions of native life, the better care of infant life, and the general improvement of living conditions as the result of education in health matters and the efforts of the excellent doctors of the race, of whom the late Hon. Sir Maui Pomare was the pioneer. Anthropologists suggest that greater social stability is also a determining factor in accounting for increases in Maori population over the last fifty years.

The amalgamation of the two races has been going on in New Zealand for more than a century, in some of the coast districts at any rate, with the result that in the Ngapuhi and Te Rarawa country of North Auckland, and to a greater extent in the South Island, the Maori population is largely half-caste. The small popu-

lation in the South Island is more than half pakeha. But the Maori element is never likely to be submerged entirely by this blending of the races. The original inhabitant of New Zealand is too strongly marked a type of humanity to lose himself altogether in the on-sweeping Anglo-Celtic tide.

That he is a virile member of the Polynesian family is sufficiently proved by the significant increase of the purely Maori factor and by the earnest efforts of numerous tribal communities to take their place alongside the pakeha in industries on the land. Sir Peter Buck (Te Rangihiroa), that distinguished authority on the Maori-Polynesian, wrote from Honolulu: "It seems to me, gazing round the Pacific from the metaphorical top of Maunaloa (in Hawaii), that the Maori race is the only one which is struggling to maintain its individuality as a race and moulding European culture to suit its requirements." We who are on the spot can appreciate the truth of Te Rangihiroa's sympathetic tribute to the endeavour of the Maori leaders and people to establish themselves socially and industrially as a power in the land, and to adjust themselves to the often troublesome ways of modern life.

The Treaty of Waitangi, which established in Englishmen's eyes the Maori right to his own country, was not conceded to him out of the pakeha's loving kindness and compassion. It was a treaty between two strong peoples, both fighting races; it was the only method whereby the Englishman could induce the Maori to accept the name of a foreign flag. Too well the pakeha pioneers in 1840 knew that they could not conquer the Maoris by force of arms and annex their lands, as had been done by English people in other lands. They were forced to conciliate the powerful tribes and to bargain for their lands instead of occupying them by right of the strong arm.

It was the strength, intelligence and military skill of the Maori that compelled the European to respect him. Some Maori land, however, was confiscated following military action, and settlement of debts, following extensive granting of credit by storekeepers, has been suggested as a means of land purchase. In the after years of war between the races it was made abundantly clear that the Maori, though defeated, could never be conquered or abased, and it was then that political rights were conferred on him. It was only Maori generosity and hospitality, conjoined to a mutual eagerness for trade, that enabled the Englishmen to gain a footing on New Zealand soil at all.

The geographical distribution of the various tribes remains very much as it was in 1840— though the Maori land areas, of course, have diminished very greatly in the course of pakeha settlement. There are changes due to the wars; Waikato, for example, lost much of the best parts of their lands by arbitrary confiscation in 1864, and there were large confiscations in Taranaki and on the East Coast of the North

Island. The geographical distribution has been changing over recent years due to resettlement of people on new farm land that has been opened up, particularly in the volcanic plateau area. Urbanisation is another factor, which is seen in the rapid increase in Maori population in the large centres.

The old hereditary lines are still held in high honour, but peaceful leadership today is chiefly seen in politics. Here the clan system, the old sense of loyalty to the ariki, still has play, modified by educational changes and the progressive influence of the younger generation.

The organisation of Maori society was based on the tribal system; in this the old New Zealander to some extent resembled the Scottish Highlander and the Red Indian. There was no united nation or commonwealth, as the European knows it. The frequent feuds kept the clans apart, except when, for temporary purposes, such as a fighting expedition, several tribes allied in descent combined for numerical strength. There was no king reigning as supreme head over the tribes. Kingship was quite foreign to the native mind until the English came, and until, in the second decade of British sovereignty, many tribes united under a great chief, forming a political confederation based on English teaching, and on lately-acquired knowledge of the outside world.

The communal system of the Maori had its obvious great advantages when any important and heavy task was to be performed. The whole strength of the tribe was at the disposal of the ariki, the sacred paramount chief; so, too, in war, the fighting leader could call on all the clansmen, for military training was universal—in fact, it was the chief pleasure and recreation of the people. Even in modern times one has seen this communal organisation at work, despite the long years of disintegration of the clan structure.

Tribes put forth the utmost efforts in preparation for great meetings; and the ancient system was turned to good account in the farming industry, although the tendency now seems to be towards greater individualism.

The Maori's mental capacity and plane of culture, like many isolated and supposedly primitive members of the human family, was high indeed. The literature of the people, unwritten until the pakeha came; the mythology, traditions and poetry handed down from generation to generation by word of mouth; the craftsmanship and decoration; the clothing, that was at once suited to climatic conditions and was so handsome and becoming—all are expressions of a strong mentality and a keen sense of the appropriate and the artistic.

The religious beliefs, the legendary lore, the vast store of song and chant, are of quite amazing volume and embody ideas that are quite as fine as examples in the classic mythology and poetry of the Old World.

The late Viscount Bledisloe, one of New Zealand's most highly respected Governors-General, who displayed such a great and generous interest in New Zealand's historic places, had given eloquent expression on many occasions to his appreciation of the Maori's character and culture.

"Each race," he said in an address in Can-

terbury at a celebration of the centenary of the Kaiapoi Pa, "can learn much from the other. If the pakeha can claim greater strenuousness, business acumen and industrial capacity (born of longer experience in an atmosphere of throbbing industry and fierce competition) the Maori can justly be credited with dogged courage, chivalry, love of nature, generous-heartedness and abounding good humour, and can at least vie with his British comrade in loyalty, dignity, refinement, athletic achievement, and eloquent speech. . . . Some hold that the process of continual amelioration of the native race can best be advanced by ever-increasing intermarriage with the pakeha. Far be it from me to deprecate such unions—many have been very happy and have greatly benefited this country. But I am confident that the Maori race can, in due course, develop all the qualities that make for the highest achievement in every walk of life without necessitating any infusion of extraneous blood, and I hope that there will be at least a strong and growing nucleus of men and women of pure Maori stock, proud of their beautiful and picturesque language, their music, their poetry and their handicrafts."

The Maori, it may be said in brief, has regained his mauri ora, his soul, his vitality, his will to live and flourish. The rapid increase of population has been accompanied by a continuing desire to retain those cultural elements which can exist in a modern world. Today, Maori is still spoken as a first language by a section of the population and more pakeha than ever before are studying Maori language and culture.

2

POLYNESIAN MIGRATIONS

The Polynesian ancestors of our Maoris, a blend of many races, were believed to be the greatest ocean rovers and navigators of ancient times. The origin of the race is a problem over which many great students of the races of mankind have exercised themselves, and a recent study suggests that drift voyaging was more significant than deliberate voyages of discovery.

A great deal has been written about ancient Asiatic immigrations into the Pacific, and some students have attempted to fix dates of the various eastward voyaging colonists from India and Malaya, Cambodia and other parts of the continent. But the difficulty of setting a period for the peopling of this vast oceanic world is apparent unless scientific methods are used. We do not know when the first waves of immigration left Asia, nor do we know where the Polynesians left the mainland to venture from island to island, ever eastward. Archae-ologists, botanists, linguists and anthropologists are tracing the Polynesian migrations back step by step, so that in time, we will be able to trace their voyaging with more certainty than we can today. The arbitrary fixing of dates is absurd when one comes to examine the races of ancient man, and to realise, however faintly, what physical changes must have occurred in the Pacific since human beings first

appeared here. It is generally believed that the islands of this ocean were peopled from Asiatic shores, although Heyerdahl believes in an American origin for the Polynesians.

The Polynesian may, with truth, be described as one of the greatest long-distance sailors in the world. Long before our European ancestors ventured out of sight of land, the ancestors of our Maoris were making voyages, whether deliberate or accidental, of thousands of miles across the world's greatest ocean with their long outrigger sailing-craft. They were seekers of new lands who long antedated the daring Norsemen or Columbus.

The Pacific was, of course, a far more favourable cruising ground than the Atlantic. From Papua in the west to the Tuamotus in the far east of the Pacific there were islands everywhere—islands high and low, islands great and small, most of them affording shelter and food of one kind or another. In the course of many centuries of short distance voyaging from one group to another, sometimes compelled by wars or increasing population to seek fresh homes, they acquired a rudimentary knowledge of navigation and seamanship that enabled them to sail back and forth with perfect confidence.

They had no scientific instruments, the mariner's compass was unknown to them, but they had their own primitive but usually sufficient means of making their way across the ocean for short distances. They used the winds, they observed the stars, they knew much of currents and tides; they could allow roughly for the leeway which their shallow-draft canoes made when sailing on a wind. They observed the flight of birds, they knew by various signs when they were nearing land, as, for example, the bright reflection in the sky of a lagoon-island still below the horizon, the glint from its dazzling calm mirror.

The sailing-craft in which the ancestors of our Maoris crossed the ocean to New Zealand were very different from the canoes of today, and those larger war canoes of the past which are preserved in the museums. They were more of the type of sea-going pahi which Cook and other navigators saw at Tahiti and many other islands of the Eastern Pacific. They could be paddled, but their crews relied mostly on sail. Some of them were fast sailing machines and with a favourable breeze could easily outsail the European ships which explored the South Seas.

They were not so long as the large canoes which the Maoris learned to make in New Zealand, where trees of great size, the kauri, totara, rimu and kahikatea, grew in vast abundance. For the keel section the largest trees procurable, which were not nearly of such length or diameter as those of this country, were hewn into canoe shape, and upon this was built up a vessel of hewn planks or slabs, wrought with great labour with stone axes, and fastened together with sinnet (coconut fibre) and strengthened with beams and ties. To this waka, as the Maoris call it, was attached an outrigger to give the craft stability.

All the large canoes had masts and sails; the latter were of matting, woven from leaves of the pandanus tree. The rig of some of the canoes somewhat resembled that of a fore-and-aft schooner, but there were no booms or gaffs. Usually, however, the craft carried one sail; a picture of a Tongan sailing canoe, probably the fastest type in the South Seas, in Cook's *Voyages* shows a large lozenge-shaped sail, apex downwards, hoisted on a comparatively short mast.

Many of the larger vessels were double canoes; this type of craft survives in the Tokelau and other islands into modern times. For long ocean voyages, however, the large strong single canoe, with outrigger, was perhaps the more seaworthy; the double canoe type was liable to disaster in rough weather. Tradition tells us that the *Tainui,* one of the most famous of the canoes which reached New Zealand some six centuries ago from Tahiti, was a single canoe. The *Arawa,* which brought the ancestors of the Rotorua tribes from Tahiti, must have been an unusually large vessel, because the legends of its voyage describe it as having had three masts.

Probably the ordinary sailing pahi, waka, or wa'a was, as a rule, not so long as the *Toki-a-Tapiri,* the historic war canoe, over eighty feet in length, which is to be seen in the War Memorial Museum in Auckland. But the outrigger would give to the island craft far more stability than the Maori canoe possesses in a sea-way. The use of the outrigger (amatiatia) was discontinued in New Zealand, where the Polynesian immigrants found so much of their canoe voyaging was in smooth water, on the rivers and lakes, and where coastwise voyagers could wait for fine weather and quiet seas. Even so, evidence has been found in New Zealand of the early Polynesian using the outrigger in these waters.

It is difficult to fix the period at which the voyages of the Pacific Islands peoples to New Zealand began. Recent archaeological dating by C^{14} means has provided us with evidence that Polynesians lived in Wairau and in the far south of New Zealand during the eleventh century. We know, from a study of the genealogies and traditions, which are memorised well in every Maori tribe, that the last great wave of Polynesian immigration was approximately six centuries ago, when many crews, brown sailors from Tahiti, Ra'iatea and Rarotonga, are said to have made landfall

along our East Coast, from the North Cape to the East Cape, and cruised about the far-extending shores until they found places in which to settle. But they found the country already populated in many parts by the descendants of earlier voyagers from Polynesia. As to the length of the voyage from the tropics, a large outrigger canoe could probably sail the distance in about the time our first schooners used to run from Tahiti and Rarotonga to Auckland. A month's sailing, making a leading wind of the south-east trade most of the way, would usually bring the Polynesian pilgrim ships down on the New Zealand coast.

Some imaginative students of things Maori have made reference to alleged Maori-Polynesian voyages to the icy South. This even found its way into history books used in the schools. According to one compiler of books, the Polynesians who made voyages of astonishing length, ventured as far as the Antarctic. This indeed would have been an astonishing voyage if it were true.

The idea of the Maori of old time, and above all the Polynesian from tropic lands, sailing southward ho! regardless of storm and cold, is obviously altogether fantastic. No Polynesian sea chief would have attempted so purposeless and insane a voyage. What the ancient island navigators hoped they might find after they set out from the tropics and sailed away south-west was a comfortable place to settle—land, and plenty of it, after their circumscribed life where the cultivable areas were too small for the increasing population. New Zealand provided them with all that they required. Probably no brown sailors of that era got further south than the Chatham Islands, the group they called Rekohu, the Abode of Fog. The voyages of our Maoris' ancestors were sufficiently wide in range and hazardous in character without taking them to the Antarctic Circle.

The story seems to have originated in a vague and misconstrued Rarotongan legend about the icy seas, quoted in one of the late S. Percy Smith's books. The author did not intend to give the impression that the Polynesian reached the Antarctic. He knew well that the old voyagers, who are supposed to have seen icebergs and sea lions, did not need to go further than the latitude of southern New Zealand. Ice has been known to have drifted as far north as the Chatham Islands in recent times, and it is quite possible that exploring crews fell in with icebergs thereabouts, but they certainly would not want to cruise any nearer to frozen seas.

Both the single and the double types of canoe had deck-houses of a kind sufficient for the purpose of shelter and rest on an ocean voyage. The spars connecting the long single canoe with the outrigger were decked, and on the planks a strongly supported thatched structure was built; and a similar house was built on the timber which decked over the greater part of the double canoes. It was possible to cook on board these vessels, on beds of sand surrounded with stones, but, of course, cooking was limited by the amount of fuel carried. Food supplies of all the island tubers and fruit could be carried. For drinking, the voyagers relied largely on coconuts, and water was carried in calabashes and in coconut-shell vessels in netted sinnet covers. A typical anchor-stone is shown on page 17.

There is a legend that on one of the principal sailing-canoes which came here from the eastern Pacific slaves were killed and eaten when the food ran short. No doubt cannibalism occurred on more than one long ocean voyage; just as it has occurred in modern times in the Pacific when white crews were adrift in open boats in a starving condition.

It is possible, according to some people, that the far-voyaging ancestors of our Maoris used a primitive kind of ocean chart. During last century, it is known that these charts were in use in the Marshall Islands, up in the north; and a trader about fifty years ago saw one in the possession of a Santa Cruz canoe captain. Santa Cruz is a small group of reef islands to the north of the New Hebrides and south-east of the Solomon Islands; its people, who are bold and skilful sailors, still make ocean passages in their outrigger canoes, covering some hundreds of miles.

One chart was a square of material like tapa cloth; fastened to it were small pieces of coral, sticks, stones, coconut shell, and other articles, indicating various islands and their relative positions. These western Pacific natives have a knowledge of the stars as guides in navigation and they preserve to this day seafaring lore that the Maori has lost. The Polynesian sailors who made voyages between the tropic islands and New Zealand were as great as the Melanesians of the Western Pacific in seamanship and they perhaps had some elementary means of estimating distance and rate of sailing. There is much confusion regarding the alleged sailing directions supposedly given by Kupe, but Sir Peter Buck summed up the position very well when he said that the Maori ancestors found their way to New Zealand despite them. Even if the Maori drifted to this country by accident, his seamanship merits the greatest admiration and his achievement is still a significant and wonderful one.

3

MAORI LIFE AND INDUSTRIES

THE NORTH ISLAND of New Zealand was believed to be largely populated when the sailing-craft of the last historic migration from Tahiti and other islands were said to have made landfall on this coast. Archaeological research in both the North and South Islands shows that the people of those times were peaceful hunters of the moa who had a material culture ancestral to that of the people we call Maori. They were Polynesians too, and the results of modern research suggests that these "Moahunters" were early Maoris. The *Tainui, Arawa, Aotea, Takitimu* and other vessels cruised from place to place along the coast until their crews found places where they could settle without coming into immediate conflict with the people of previous migrations.

The fact that the *Tainui*—a whole bookful of history and song has been written about that famous canoe—did not remain on the shores of the Hauraki Gulf or Waitemata Harbour, but was dragged across the Tamaki-Manukau portage and went on down the West Coast, is sufficient traditional indication in itself that there was a considerable population on the plain where Auckland City now stands, and around the Gulf.

It is not at all likely that those sea-weary immigrants would have continued their search for new homes had this most desirable part of the country been unoccupied. But tradition says that the tangata-whenua, the people of the land, the aborigines, by whatever tribal name they were known, were numerous and strong, and forcible dispossession was out of the question. *Tainui* moved on and later, by "peaceful penetration" sometimes, and sometimes by force of arms—rau-patu, the blade of the weapon—they gained the upper hand of their predecessors in the land. So with the other ancestral ships.

Consider now the life of the various peoples in this new land, so abounding in food, though without the spontaneous growth of the tropics. We may picture the inhabitants of a village leaving each morning to the day's work of tending the cultivations or fishing in sea or river or snaring and spearing the birds that teemed in the bush.

The planting and harvesting of the kumara and taro crops were undertakings for the whole community and were carried out with much ceremony and attention to the laws of tapu and all the ancient ritual for the propitiation of the deities of the food gardens. The forests were full of birds for the villagers with their snaring tackle, and their slender timber spears, which were sometimes thirty feet in length.

Some of the snares, those for the kaka parrots, were elbowed perches of wood, placed in the tops of rata and other trees frequented by the birds, which were caught by the feet in a running tackle twitched by the hunter in the branches below. Pigeon and tui were caught in great numbers in another kind of snare, set above water-filled troughs like miniature canoes; they were entangled in these when they settled to drink. Wild duck and teal, so abundant on the streams and lakes, lagoons and swamps, were taken in great numbers with slip-knot nooses, often made of growing rushes, among the water channels through the reeds. Often in the season when the berries of the many small trees were ripe, and the fruit of such fresh trees as the kahikatea pine and the miro and tawa were ripe, the whole village or tribe went into the bush for the capture of the kaka, pigeon, tui and bellbird.

But it was chiefly in the sea-fisheries that the Maori of old time rejoiced. The people would camp on the seashore for many weeks in the summer season and engage in the chase of the shark and the hauling of the long seine nets (kupenga) for the many kinds of edible fish. Shark, snapper, cod, grouper, kahawai and mullet were taken in great quantities and much was sun-dried and smoke-dried for future use. On the beaches of a thousand sheltered bays long lines of shark hung drying in the sun in the hot days of summer and diffusing all around an aroma agreeable to Maori nostrils. The shark were taken with hook and line, and although the Maori did not fish for the sport of the thing but for the pot (or rather, the hangi, the earth steam-oven), there was often an exciting fight with the shark tribe which delighted the warrior soul. The mako shark of

the Bay of Plenty was sought for the sake of its triangular teeth, which were prized as ear pendants, for men as well as women.

Then there were the shellfish to be gathered everywhere about the coast, each tribe always keeping within its carefully defined bounds— oysters (tio), mussels (kuku and purewha), cockles (pipi). All this food of the salt sea was covered by the term "kai-mataitai", which included every form of edible sea-food from sharks to cockles and a seaweed called karengo. The inland tribes in some cases had access to the sea as a fishing reserve, but often they bartered bush food, preserved birds packed in bark containers, to the sea-coast people for salty "kai-mataitai", which they craved.

Certain bush berries, too, were on the list of foods, though they were not so easily obtainable, or so delicious, as the fruits of the tropic islands. The large blue drupes of the tawa tree, very resinous of flavour if tasted raw, were split and sun-dried on flat rocks until they became palatable. The karaka berry, large and orange-coloured, was eaten; the kernel was poisonous until it was treated by steeping and drying it. The sweet fruit of the white pine (kahikatea) was relished by children quite as much as by the bush pigeons. Parts of the nikau palm pith, and the korau and mamaku fern tree, were eaten. The young shoots of other ferns, called generally pikopiko, were cooked and eaten. In one way and another the Maori found abundance to sustain life, though he had to work harder to obtain it in these islands than in Tahiti, Rarotonga or Samoa.

When the first Europeans came in their exploring ships the people obtained two important items that became their chief food supply —pigs and potatoes. Maize, too, was introduced and it was largely cultivated throughout the North Island.

The Maori was an industrious and skilful agriculturist, though his operations were limited in pre-European times to the sweet potato, the yam and taro and a vegetable marrow. When potatoes, maize and wheat were introduced, his field was enlarged, and there was a time, in the beginning of British colonisation here, when the towns were dependent to a large extent on the Maori farmers for their food supplies.

The position today with many Maoris is that they are almost, or quite, landless and the obligation lies on the country to provide them with sufficient of their native soil for a living. However, under the present vigorous and progressive native administration, Maori farming has been re-established on a modern basis. The co-operative tribal system under which the people worked well of old has been given a new and excellent application. Groups of people have been established on undeveloped land, under the oversight of the Maori Affairs Department, with expert assistance.

Teams of young Maoris have been set to work at breaking in and cultivating the land, and during the last few years great improvements have been made, and hundreds of families have been settled on holdings of their own on which they are able to carry on dairying and other farm activities. The amount of land available, however, is still not enough for the growing population, many of whom are forced to seek opportunities in the larger centres.

There are Maori-supplied dairy factories and the best of dairy herds; on the East Coast, sheep-farming is carried on on a large scale. A new spirit has been infused into the race, or rather, it would be more correct to say the ancient spirit of industry has been revived and given new shape. The moving spirit in the farming enterprise, and the establishment of the people in comfortable homes on the soil of their ancestors, was the late Sir Apirana Ngata, the Maori Minister, who, after seeing his own tribe, Ngati-Porou, of the East Coast, well on its way to prosperity and independence as sheep-farmers and owners of dairy herds, and producers of butter and cheese, meat and wool, proceeded to organise the other tribes on similar progressive lines. He made use of the tribal organisation and traditions to inspire the people to adapt themselves to modern conditions in a spirit of healthy rivalry.

"In dealing with the Maori we must proceed tribally," Sir Apirana explained. The ancient community system under some trusted leader, usually hereditary, was a power for good which contact with white civilisation had

affected. This olden spirit is now partially revived, and legislation during the last five decades has been based largely on the tribal system which encouraged persistence in industrious effort. So the Maori is moving onward, with courage and determination, to the best kind of life, not only the farming of his native land on level terms with the pakeha, but also in the professional and commercial fields, where he is steadily making his mark.

4

RELIGION, MYTHOLOGY AND SACRED LORE

IT IS ONLY within comparatively recent years that the religious system of the Maori-Polynesian has come to be understood and appreciated by students of comparative religions and mythology. The early missionaries, and many later writers, dismissed the Maori religion as mere superstition, and this narrow and uninformed view was held until sympathetic students of the race obtained a true insight into the subject and came to realise the beauty and nobility of much of its sacred lore, preserved so carefully by the chiefs and priests. The missionaries discouraged all the ancient beliefs; it was, as they conceived it, their duty to replace all the "heathen" faiths with the Rongo-pai, the "Glad tidings".

In this process of changing a people's outlook on matters spiritual, the good people of the missions destroyed much that was of great worth, not only in an ethnological sense, but in the preservation of the people's interest in life and will to live. The belief in tapu, or the forbidden, for example, was not quite the senseless and absurd superstition that those Europeans who first encountered it represented it to be. It had its definite value as a salutary prohibition, and as a corrective to the exercise of brute force. Tapu could be abused, like every other institution, but it had a certain moral force. The fear of makutu, or witchcraft, the only defence of the weak against the strong-minded, also operated as a deterrent to force.

The Maori religion had its roots in nature worship and veneration of ancestors. There is something that is sublime in the Maori-Polynesian cosmogony, the recital of successive phases in the evolution of light from darkness, the evolution of man through various stages down to the ancestral Tiki, the first human being. The earliest names on the great gene-alogy are descriptive of the gradual emergence of human life from the cosmic gloom and chaos. Then there are the names of the primal deities which personify the mighty forces of nature.

Rangi is the Sky, the male parent of all things. Papa is the Earth, the receptive and productive mother of all created things. The winds and storms are personified as Tawhiri-matea. Tangaroa is the God of Ocean, the ruler of the sea and all the life that is therein. It was natural that in many parts of Oceania, the myriad isles of the Pacific, Tangaroa should be the most revered God of all. Tane is the God of Fertility. He is the source of all life, and especially of all growing things; and another form is Tane-Mahuta, the God of the Forests. Rongo, the personification of peace and cultivation of food, is associated with Tane, and the two are often jointly addressed in prayers and chants. Ru, in full Ruwaimoko, or Ruaumoko, is the force of earthquakes and volcanoes and all the powers of the underworld. He is the youngest born (or, as is sometimes heard in tradition, the unborn) child of Papa-tuanuku, and he feeds upon and consumes the breast of his mother, the Earth. This is a poetic way of describing the action of volcanoes.

And then comes Tu, the god of mankind and of war; Tu of many attributes, the angry-faced, the red-belted, the god invoked by warriors on the battle trail.

Above and beyond all these and the many other deities in the Maori-Polynesian pantheon, there was the belief in some mysterious all-powerful First Cause. This was Io, the supreme god whose heavens were twelve. Io-mata-ngaro —Io of the Hidden Face—the name in full, was not for the common tongue; the great name must not be mentioned lightly. The familiarity with which the Supreme Deity is addressed by many a glib pakeha preacher would have seemed strange and unbecoming to the high priest of old-time Maoridom. The name was not used in the ordinary karakia for the purpose of ordinary life, recited by the family or tribal tohungas; it was the higher order of priest only who addressed or invoked Io.

Earth-magic, forest-magic, was strong in the heart of the Maori. The supernatural was ever with him in his daily life. It impinged closely on his waking and sleeping hours; it strongly coloured his thoughts; it entered into all his actions. Everything was contingent in some respect or other on the approval of his gods. Familiar spirits, invisible presences were round about him; atua and kehua, deities and ghosts, all manner of dread and uncanny beings, and it was ever necessary to propitiate them by ritual observances. One of the widely held beliefs was, and is still, the faith in the gift of

second sight, or mata-kite. The clairvoyant sense displayed by so many Maoris is one of the faculties which the Celt and the New Zealander possess in common.

All nature was alive; the soil was the Earth-Mother, Papa-tuanuku; the tree was the embodiment of Tane-Mahuta, the deity of the forest. A great tree was not felled for canoe-making or house-building without religious observances; the Father of the Woods must be

propitiated and conciliated lest he resent the axeman's work. The ancient ritual of the Maori persisted quietly alongside the ritual of the pakeha church; the Maori, like a wise man, adopted everything that seemed to present a chance of making his peace with the unseen world.

The Christianised Maori of today is liberal in his support of his Churches. The strongest sect is the Church of England, with the Church of Ratana another numerous sect with many adherents. Ratana was a faith-healer of great mana in the Rangitikei district, who founded a Church of his own and established a large religious and industrial settlement. Many of his followers are industrious farmers and there are large cultivations on the large estate which is seen on the way from Wellington to Wanganui.

A religious faith with a dramatic history is the Ringatu, which may be described as the patriotic Church of the Maori. Ringa-tu means "Uplifted hand", or "Raised hand", and the name is a continual reminder to the adherents of the faith of its origin, in the midst of blood and fire in Taranaki ninety years ago. The ritual of the religion, which has a few thousand followers, is based on the form of service framed by the rebel leader Te Kooti, but the original inspiration came from the Pai-marire, or Hauhau cult invented by Te Ua, the fanatic prophet, which gave a new and more desperate turn to the wars in 1864. Te Kooti, in framing his service, when in exile as a political prisoner on Chatham Island in 1867-1868, discarded the Pai-marire pidgin-English chants and made use chiefly of the Psalms and other books of the Old Testament.

The result was an inspiring form of worship resembling the Church of England service with some essentially Maori features. Te Kooti called his religion the Wairua-Tapu, or Holy Spirit, but the old, historic name Ringatu is the designation chiefly used today. The gesture which gave its name to the faith, too, persists to this day. Te Ua taught his followers to hold up the right hand, palm outwards, on a level with the face, when they repeated the incantations, and to say "Hapa! Pai-marire! Hau!" when they faced the white soldiers in battle, with upraised hand. "Hapa" means to avert, or ward off, or pass over; the belief was that the magic word and action would prevent bullets striking the faithful. And, through all the changing fortunes of the Maori, and the various phases and modifications of the religion which fused many tribes together in a holy war against the pakeha, the sign of the uplifted hand remains as a symbol of devotion.

At Ringatu services in the Urewera Country in recent times, just as on the King Country

border in the 'eighties, one has seen the wor-
shippers, in their responses, hold the right hand
up on a level with the face. So, too, as in other
Churches, the Ringatu is seen in the minister's
gesture of blessing. There is much beauty in
these services, and much that appeals to the
imagination, particularly in the evening gathering in a village meeting-house or social room
whare-puni, such as those along the Bay of
Plenty and back in the ranges, where the half-
light and primitive surroundings and the
responses and chants taken up in turn by the
dimly-seen groups of people, give a peculiar
thrill to the scene and the act of worship.

The Ringatu Church was given official recognition by the Government many years ago,
and its ministers have the legal status of those
of other Churches in the performance of
marriage. The headquarters of the sect are at
Wainui, on the shore of Ohiwa Harbour, where
it has been endowed with the block of land
occupied by Te Kooti for several years before
his death in 1893. The Church is well organ-
ised; it has exercised a definite influence for the
betterment of the people along the Bay of

Plenty and in other parts of the country where
its adherents are numerous.

THE TOHUNGA

The tohunga was the priestly adept, the wise
man of the old generation. In him was reposed
the profoundest knowledge of the tribe's
religion, mythology and history. (The tohunga
illustrated on page 24 is holding a rakau whaka-
papa, a carved stick that was the key to the
tribal genealogy.)

As an example of the tohunga maori, let
me describe the chief and priest Tauke, of the
Ngati-Ruanui tribe, Taranaki. He died at
Hokorima, on the Waimate Plain, in 1916, at
the age of about eighty-seven years. Tauke was
a man of unusual parts, and his sometimes
stormy life was closely intertwined with New
Zealand's Ten Years' War and the troubled
political history of the West Coast. To his last
day he held strongly to his clannish patriotism;
he had shed his blood in defence of the Maori
nationality as he and his compatriots conceived
it about ninety years ago. He was a fighting-
chief and war-priest and in his days of peace

he revived a kind of lodge of instruction in esoteric Maori lore, while at the same time, singularly, spending hours daily in poring over the pakeha scriptures.

Taranaki peak swelled up grandly to the soaring spearhead of glistening white, framed between the forest trees, on the north of Hokorima Village, where I called to talk with Tauke one day. It looked, as it might well be, the Mountain God of these passionately patriotic clansfolk. It was on the green turfy marae in front of Tauke's house that I found the old man sitting, with a coloured blanket girt round his waist, his white head bare, intent on reading the ecstatic visions of the Dreamer in "Nga Whakakitenga", or Revelation, in a fifty-year-old copy of the Bible. The old man laid his book aside and took off his glasses. He looked the mystic that he was: white as Egmont's snowy peak, calm but deep penetrating eyes looking out under white-bushed buttresses of brows. One of his hands was scarred and mutilated, the thumb and part of a finger missing. "That happened at Te Morere", he said. Te Morere was Sentry Hill, one of the frontier posts of the British military forces. Tauke was one of the band of Hauhau warriors, strong in their fanatic faith, who attacked the redoubt in 1864, only to be beaten back with fifty of their number killed and scores wounded; and later Tauke fought all through the bush wars up to 1869.

Tauke was the last of the tohungas of the Ngati-Ruanui tribe. He was a seer, a dreamer, and he was the instructor of the tribal whare-maire, the school of legend and tradition, religious ritual and genealogical recitals; for the Taranaki people are conservative and cherish the ancient faiths at heart; it is right that they should. Many years ago Tauke married a young couple with the ceremonies of his Polynesian forefathers. A Maori who was present described to me the remarkable rites; for the ritual Tauke went to the very primitive prayers and recitals; a priest of nature.

The scene was the tribal meeting-house. The near relatives of the young man and woman were gathered there. The low door and window were closed, and in the half-darkness—though it was in the daytime—with a wizardly small fire burning at the foot of the central house pillar, casting a flickering light on the carved figures on the wall slabs and on the scroll-painted rafters, Tauke recited the old old prayers that invoked Rangi and Papa, the Sky-Father and Earth-Mother, and besought fruitfulness for the lovers. The karakia ended, the couple, at his bidding, began their wedded life there and then.

It was perhaps in keeping with the medley of ancient and modern in Tauke's character and history that the burial of the sage of Ngati-Ruanui, in 1916, should have been preceded by a poi dance by the women of Parihaka, their hair decked with waving white feathers, and that the old man of the forest and the plains should have been laid to rest to the high chants of the ancient times and the rhythmic action-song of the *Aotea,* his grand ancestral canoe from Hawaiki.

5

MAORI LANGUAGE AND LITERATURE

THE TONGUE OF THE MAORI is not difficult to learn, but as with all living languages it cannot be learned from books. The niceties of pronunciation, the idioms, the manner of expression, can only be acquired by personal contacts and conversation, and there are grammars and dictionaries and phrase-books to supplement the oral instruction.

The construction of the language is simple and yet scientific; its beauty may be gathered from many printed sources. The early missionaries who gave Maori its written form deserve the gratitude of New Zealanders of both races for the phonetic alphabet and the avoidance of incorrect spelling which is current in some other parts of the Pacific. In particular, the "nga" sound is given its proper value in our Maori spelling. It is otherwise in many South Sea groups, where the missionaries adopted an arbitrary "g" to represent the "ng", with the consequence of grotesque, incorrect pronunciation of native names, such as Pangopango (American Samoa), which is confusingly spelled "Pagopago", and inevitably pronounced "Paygo-paygo" by travellers and other strangers who encounter the name.

Once the Maori vowel sounds with their long and short values are learned, there is no difficulty in pronouncing Maori. The right accenting of the syllables in a word is acquired by experience. There are only fifteen letters in the written language and the task of learning is correspondingly simplified. There is no *g* sound in Maori, apart from the *ng,* and there is no b, c, d, f, j, l, q, s, v, x, y or z. Maori is far more scientific in its construction than English, and as Hare Hongi wrote of it, "here you have no borrowing from fortuitous sources but a tongue at once comprehensive, ample in all required processes and proudly self-reliant."

That remark applies, of course, to the tongue in its purity, uncontaminated by hybridised words.

Nowadays, current Maori, spoken and written, contains a great many words which are simply Maori equivalents of English words. There are hundreds of words which look Maori but which are English, as pronounced by the Maori. Examples are reta (letter), pepa (paper), motoka (motor car), hate (shirt), witi (wheat), e rima heneti (five cents), and the list is ever being added to. Curious transliterated Maori is manufactured in this way, as whakitarata (foxtrot), kapureihana (corporation). Such publications as the Government Maori Gazette are unavoidably full of expressions for which there is no Maori equivalent and which therefore are the English words

phonetically Maorified. In another publication, a small Maori newspaper, I noted the remarkable word "kakatu", in reference to a Maori farm on the Bay of Plenty Coast. The context gave a clue to the meaning in this association; it was "cockatoo", Australianese for a small farmer. But really "kakatu" was an apposite and clever adoption of an Australian idiom, for kaka is the Maori bush parrot, and tu means to stand. "Paamu kakatu" is, therefore, a piece of modern language quite worth preserving as a kind of Maori pun.

But the tongue in its unspoiled beauty is a subject which every New Zealander should endeavour to cultivate to some extent, even if the study does not proceed beyond the pronunciation of Maori words and names. It is quite easy to acquire this degree of knowledge, and a little pain devoted to it will enable the student to avoid the barbarous mutilation of familiar names that one hears every day. Beautiful names are often rendered grotesque by mispronunciation. How often one hears public speakers and radio lecturers fumble native place names or confidently place the accents on the wrong syllables!

Often the pakeha residents of a place are the offenders. I have heard Whenuakite called "Fenugit" and Poroti pronounced as "Porrerty". Punakitere (a beautiful North Auckland name meaning swift-flowing fountain, or river-source) is locally called something like "Pennaker-tree". Patumahoe becomes in some pakeha mouths "Pettermaho," with stress on the "ho". Wellington's seaside suburb Muritai customarily has a "mew" put into it by its residents, not knowing the elementary fact that the letter "u" is pronounced "oo" in Maori. Ahipara, a Far North place name, becomes "Hy-prer"; it is quite easy to give it its proper sound. It is necessary to note the right accenting of words and place names. The unschooled pakeha invariably places the stress on the wrong syllable; he has a perfect genius for getting it wrong. So also with the long and short vowel sounds. Tapu is a sufficiently well-known word, yet one often hears it pronounced "tar-pu", with the emphasis on the long "tar", whereas both vowels should be sounded short.

Sufficient now to recommend the study of the tongue, if only to be able to pronounce New Zealand place names and comprehend something of their meaning.

Turn now to a consideration of some features of the very large and very fascinating field that lies open in the literature, legend and poetry of the race.

The old school tohungas and learned men have gone, but the tales of the ancients, the history of the tribes, the astronomical and natural history lore, the classic poetical compositions with which their minds were stored, have by no means perished with them. The Maori has—or had until pakeha schools made him dependent on printed books—a marvellous memory and a passion for repeating songs, genealogies, tribal traditions and proverbial sayings. He knows his forefathers better than the average European knows his. He is proud of his long ancestral line, every name of which he can repeat, often for scores of generations—and upon occasion he has invented an ancestor where a link was missing, as Maori Land Court judges knew full well. Every tribe is versed in its own history for centuries past, and naturally has a considerable acquaintance with that of its neighbours and old-time enemies.

Old songs are treasured and sung again and again—songs dating from a remote antiquity and containing allusions to events which occurred long before the Maori left the South Sea Islands for New Zealand. At Maori meetings today one will hear chants of antique structure and archaic wording, as different from the sadly Anglicised Maori tongue of today as Chaucer's English is from the diction of a Member of Parliament. To many Maoris the classical and mythological allusions contained in the songs and proverbs of old are as much a sealed book as they are to the average European. But in every tribe there are men and women who can afford assistance to the Maori student in the explanation of these things, who pride themselves on their knowledge of olden tales and poems, and to whom nothing can give greater annoyance than to hear their treasured songs and traditions perverted or misunderstood.

There is still a field for competent research and investigation among the Maoris, modernised in some ways though they be. For still they are Maoris at heart. In times of excitement and stress, in the hour of bereavement and calamity, the old, old spirit appears. Little incidents in proof occur now and then. The law of tapu is not without observance in certain districts even today. Instances of survivals of old beliefs are the incantations to remove the tapu from a newly-built carved house, after the olden ritual of the Maori. The pure or whakanoa ceremony (really the lifting of quarantine) is still occasionally practised, with certain modern variations.

In the Land Court minute books there are many thousands of pages of history, from the lips of well-informed natives. The native tribal councils, representative of the different canoes of the historic migration from Hawaiki, realise the importance of preserving their history. The heads of the Ngati-Maniapoto tribe of the King Country, some years ago compiled a complete genealogy of the tribe, dating back for many generations anterior to the migration from the Society Islands and

Rarotonga. And besides history pure and simple there are folk stories and poems innumerable to be heard and noted in every village by those who know the language.

The fine symbolism of Maori mythology will be found worthy of comparison with that of the Greeks and Romans. The Maori, moreover, has all the mysticism and imagination of the Celt. There is more than a strain of the Ossianic in his poetry, in his figurative laments and wild tangi-songs. Domett interpreted the New Zealander in his eloquent way, in his *Ranolf and Amohia;* still he does not reveal to us the real Maori. That has been done since his day by those of us who have studied the Maori for a lifetime—the Maori as he is with all his virtues, faults and inconsistencies, with the strange old faiths and convictions of which he cannot divest himself, like his pakeha ways and manners, with his clothes.

One special value of Maori history and legend is its local interest, the colour of romance which it gives to many a place in these islands of ours. There is hardly a spot— at any rate in the North Island—that has not some native tale attaching to it—not a mountain, lake or stream that has not its memories of the roving fighting Maori. We have only to look to the old countries of the world to gauge the value of these place-stories.

But no country could be richer in these raw materials for the writer than New Zealand. What Scott's novels have done for the Highlands, what Fenimore Cooper's romances and Longfellow's and Whittier's poems have done for America, the Maori clan-stories and folk-tales, the poetic origins of many place names, and the chronicles of the wars will do for our own country. The thought should be a stimulus to young New Zealanders to learn the Maori language, as their elders did who recorded the stories and poems of the now vanished wise men. That work of the past is one of the happiest memories of one's life—the days and nights spent in listening to the old legends, the epics of tribal conquest and defeat, exploration and place-naming, adventure and battle, and the play of all the human passions that made romance in his world. Thus it was that one came to understand the love of country and wild freedom that led the Maori to defy for years the white man's government, the passionate savage fight for a lost nationality. Now the bitterness of racial feeling is dead, though the pride in brave deeds remains. And knowing him through his story and song we are able to arrive at a truer and more sympathetic estimate of our fellow-countryman, the Maori.

The Poetry of the Maori

An eye for the beautiful in nature, a love of one's country, and of every hillock, grove and stream, were strong in the Maori. A chief held as a prisoner sang as he gazed over the gleaming stretch of a broad river:

> Rippling there are the
> Waters of Waikato;
> Separated am I from the
> Land of my childhood
> By the fast-flowing tide.
> Waters of Kawhia!
> O, far are you from me;
> Long severed I stand here.
> As swift flows the river
> So down fall my tears.

As with the songs of Scotland and Ireland, the soul of the people was expressed in songs of sadness and pathos. The chants and laments for the dead form a very large section, and the finest, of the poetic lore of the Maori. The soul of the race was laid bare at tangihanga or funeral ceremonies, and in messages of sorrow to bereaved ones. This is a portion of an ancient waiata tangi, or lament, by a father for his two sons:

Lonely I sit, my throbbing heart is rent
For you, my children.
  O, my sons!
My head is bent beneath my load of grief,
Like Tane's offspring, yonder fronded trees;
For you, my sons, I'm bowed
As droops the mamaku fern tree.

Where are you now? Where those happy
  youths?
The ever-ebbing tide has borne them far away.

Upon this wooded plain I rest, I mourn;
Let it be barren—let every bud be blighted;

Let not the sun above me light it with its rays,
Nor yonder mountain shelter it.
The mountains by our village home which
    shared our joys,
And warded off the harsh south breeze.

By the dread monster Whiro ye are bound
Within the dark dread house.
How busy is the multitude?
But whate'er is said or done I heed not now,
All—all is blank to me.

Why shines not now the moon?
Has it been cast from out the sky?
Those mighty cliffs, who hurled them from
    their height?
My tender plants, why did ye perish?
What deep offence have we committed that the
    gods
Should so afflict us? That their hands
Should join to make us desolate
And blot us from creation like the moa?

A poem celebrated among the Maoris is a
song composed in 1846 by Iwikau Te Heuheu,
of South Taupo, a lament for his elder brother,
the great chief Te Heuheu Tukino, who was
overwhelmed with fifty of his tribe in a land-
slide at Te Rapa, near Tokaanu. This is a
translation of the waiata:

See o'er the peak of gloomy Tauhara
The first red beams of morning glow,
Perhaps in yonder shining cloud
My lost one comes again.
        Alas, thou'rt gone!

Go, O thou mighty one, our sheltering tree!
Our guardian from the dangers of the world!
By strange and evil gods thou art o'erwhelmed.
Sleep on, O brother, in that dark abode,

And hold within thy grasp that weapon rare
Bequeathed to thee by thy renowned sire.

But turn to me again that noble form,
And let me see thy skin deep-carved with lines
Of blue; and let me see thy face
So chiselled into scrolls of beauty;
Ah, thy people now are sad and comfortless.

Faintly now gleam all the heavenly ones,
The great stars Atutahi and Rehua have
    vanished
From our sight, and that fair star that shone
Beside the Milky Way. Emblems these
        Of thee, my brother!

Lonely stands Tongariro in the south,
The rich plumes of our grand ancestral ship
The Arawa are scattered on the wave,
And weeping women wail the last lament.

Why hast thou left behind these cherished
    treasures
Of thy renowned ancestor Rongomai
And wrapped thyself in night?

Cease now thy slumber, O thou son of Rangi!
Arise and grasp thy battle-club and tell
The people of the coming days! Recite the
    omens,
Portents of war, and tell them of the foe
On-rushing like the waves of ocean,
And how thy warriors shall avenge their wrongs
Nor shrink from danger. But let thy people
Breathe awhile, nor madly covet death.

Lo! Thou art fallen; the cold earth
Receives thee as its prey.
But thy glory ne'er shall perish,
Forever it shall live, resounding o'er the
    heavens.

The Legend of the Fairy Wife

This folk-story of the Taranaki tribes serves as an example of the endless store of legends, poetic and romantic. It is very ancient and is said to have originated with the tangata-whenua, the earliest inhabitants of the country.

Te Niniko was the name of a man who lived very long ago. He was a handsome young man much given to games and dances and all kinds of enjoyment. A girl of the turehu, or patupaiarehe tribes, the fairy folk, saw him engaged in dancing and was immediately stricken with deep love for him. She herself was the most beautiful of all the fairies. Te Niniko lived in a house built a little distance from the village of his relatives and friends.

One night the fairy girl visited Te Niniko, and so charmed was he with her beauty that he made her his wife. Te Niniko wished to show his lovely wife to his people, but to this the fairy would never consent. She disappeared every morning as daylight drew near, only to return at nightfall. Te Niniko unceasingly urged his wife to show herself to his people, for he was very proud of her beauty. At last she said to him: "Wait until my child is born, and then we will introduce it to our relatives."

But Te Niniko did not heed this wish, and he boasted to his people of the beautiful wife he possessed. The people demanded to see her at once and ascertain the truth of the story. Te Niniko replied: "You cannot do that for she leaves me every morning before dawn. There is only one way to accomplish your wish; if you stop up every chink in the house through which daylight can enter, then she will not know it is morning, and will linger on awaiting it."

His people agreed, and silently in the night they filled every chink through which light could penetrate into the whare. The fairy wife came, she slept on by Niniko's side, on into the daylight hours, until long after the people were out of their dwellings; they were assembled to see her revealed to them.

Then suddenly they pulled off the mat coverings around the walls and opened the sliding door and window and sunlight flooded the place. The lovely fairy rushed out, only to be confronted by all the wondering people.

Overcome with whakama (shame, shyness and grief) and resenting bitterly the trick which had been played on her, she called up her supernatural powers to her aid, and vanished from the people's sight. Just for a few moments she stayed while she sang a tearful lament to her husband. Then a friendly mist enveloped her, and she was borne away for ever, back to the mysterious realms of the enchanted folk of the forest, and never again did the grief-stricken Niniko gaze upon his fairy wife.

6

THE MAORI IN WAR

EVERY MAN in the Maori community of old was a soldier, trained from boyhood in all the arts of defence and offence. Military training was the greatest recreation, military efficiency the source of highest pride. The Maori was a military field engineer of skill and resourcefulness. He defended his villages with elaborate earthworks and palisades; he scarped and trenched and stockaded every natural feature that offered itself as a suitable fort-site. There are not merely hundreds, but thousands, of such entrenched and terraced hills in the North Island, monuments to a wonderfully industrious and intelligent warrior race.

There was no more mobile fighter than the Maori. He was a perfect bush warrior, adept in the laying of ambuscades and planner of surprises. In the cannibal era he literally lived on his foes when out on the warpath. He ate up the stored food crops of the enemy, and then, if he were successful, ate the planters of these crops. No wagon loads of provisions were required—even had there been wagons and provisions and roads whereon to haul them.

When the introduction of the musket, more than a century ago, changed the conditions of warfare, the pa-defender adapted his defensive methods accordingly; he dug his ditch inside instead of outside the palisade, he loop-holed and flax-masked his wooden walls, and flanked his trenches with bastions for enfilading fire. Later, when the British artillery battered his stout puriri stockades and shells burst in his huts, he dug himself in as skilfully as any European field tunneller of this twentieth century.

Te Rauparaha practised approach by sap in the siege of Kaiapoi Pa in 1831, long before ever a pakeha campaign was launched in New Zealand; and Kawiti and Pene Taui in the North Auckland war of 1845 reinforced a stockading impregnable to grenadiers' bayonets with trench systems in which they could defy the British guns that pounded away at them at a range of a few hundred yards. In 1864 the really weak position at Orakau, a mere earthwork with trenches and pits, resisted attack for three days; and the burrows and frail parapets of the Gate Pa, a mere travesty of a fort compared with the massive works of an earlier era, made a shelter in which a few

hundred warriors put a British naval and military force to the right-about. The secret lay in the skilful maze of pits and trenches and the confusion caused by the sudden reappearance of Maoris in the rear of British troops after apparently being forced back.

That the modern young Maori was as good a soldier as his fighting father and grandfather was abundantly proved during both world wars. He was fully the equal of his ancestors in fortitude and endurance. He was no degenerate, softened by the peaceful life. He enlisted with a will and learned his drill quickly, and on the field did everything with a rush and immense determination.

The Maori Contingent in the First World War was recognised as a Pioneer Battalion after its service at Gallipoli in 1915, and served in France and Flanders until the end of the War. The total of all ranks who served during that time was 2,227. During the Second World War, the Maori Battalion made a name for itself as a renowned fighting unit. After the famous battles in Greece and Crete they fought gallantly in North Africa and Italy.

As a type of the grand old fighting race I cannot do better, I think, than describe one of my Arawa acquaintances of long ago, who exemplified the military fire and efficiency of the Maori—one who was in his day and generation a perfect fighting man. This was Te Araki te Pohu, a chief of Ngati-Tu sub-tribe, of Owhatiura, near Rotorua.

He was a very old man when I first knew him, a relic of the cannibal age who survived into the early years of this century. Even when he was over ninety he was still erect of figure, a tall lean man with the square shoulders of a soldier; greatly tattooed of face, and of commanding warrior presence. I have seen him working away in his potato garden, or sitting mending a fishing net, when the younger and able-bodied men of his hapu were away at the races or a football match somewhere.

He had long outlived all his comrades. It was curious to hear him speak of celebrated fighting chiefs under whom he had fought, who had been dead for half-a-century or more. Such memories roused him from his calmly introspective, half-humorous outlook on life.

His eyes would glitter, his muscle-knotted fists clench, and out would pour a narrative terse and fiery, with gestures to give point to the tale, and now and again a rhythmic snatch of a haka, or war chant, to which he had many a time danced the earth-shaking peruperu.

His was a wonderful head and face, that ancient warrior's. He had the fine eyes of the mystic, and the keen Jewish-like hawk-nose, the ihu-kaka, or "parrot-nose", as the Maoris call it, that so curiously persists among some Arawa families. He looked the patriarch, with his long snowy hair and beard, which heightened by contrast the blue-black lines of tattoo that thickly and deeply scrolled his face.

The Old Man of Owhatiura was living history, a human relic of the Stone Age. He was born probably about the year 1813, before a vestige of European civilisation had penetrated to the interior of New Zealand. He was the very last of the cannibal warriors of the Arawa. He was reared in the midst of scenes of war, and as soon as he could carry and use spear and sharp-edged stone club he was out with the older braves on the fighting trail. He told me of his long-ago war expeditions. He served in half-a-score of battles in inter-tribal warfare and, sitting there on his whariki mat, under the shade of a willow-tree, at his lakeside home, he tallied off these expeditions on his fingers.

"There was Maketu and there was Te Tumu. There was Mataipuku, near Rotorua Lake, where we fought a great fight with musket and tomahawk with the Ngati-Haua and Waikato invaders. There was Matamata, where we carried the war into the enemy's country. There was Okarea, in the Urewera Country, and there were other sieges and ambuscades. And the dead of the enemy, you ask, what became of them? Why," pointing to his mouth and grinning through his black mask of moko a humorous old grin, "Why, we ate them. Why should we waste them? I ate them! And then, in after years, I served on the side of the White Queen against the Hauhaus, in skirmishes on the coast and in the depth of the bush."

In detail Te Araki told the story of the Arawa army's storming of Te Tumu pa on the Bay of Plenty coast between Tauranga and Maketu. That was in 1836. He had a blanket

round his shoulders over his shirt, but he threw it off and give it a twist around his waist for freer arm action in his dramatic narrative.

"When we all assembled at Ohinemutu for our expeditions," he said "we danced a great war-dance and the thunder of our leaping parade shook the ground. It was a great war-party, the full fighting strength of the Rotorua tribes. We marched down to the coast, and cautiously by night, approached the palisaded fort Te Tumu, on a low sandy mound near the beach.

"Just at the break of day we dashed at the stockade. Our foes, the Ngaiterangi, though few in number, fought desperately. But at last we forced our way through and over the war-fence. There was I, hacking away with my long-handled tomahawk—like this! Many of the defenders fled in the direction of Tauranga, but we pursued them along the beach and killed or captured most of them. So fell that fort, they died, they were cooked, they were eaten! *(Ka hinga taua pa, ka mate, ka hangia, ka kai!)* There lay the Fish-of-Whiro, the slain warriors. After the battle and pursuit we gathered in the conquered pa, the many hundreds of the Arawa, and there we danced our war-dance of jubilation and victory.

"This was the chorus we shouted as we held our weapons horizontally before us with both hands and quickly raised them at arms' length above our heads—like this—and down again in time to the song:

> "Koia ano!
> Koia ano!
> Koia ano te peruperu!
> Inahoki ra te taiaroa,
> Whakatirohia mai na
> Ki te whana.
> A-ha! Pare-rewha,
> Pare-rewha,
> Pare-rewha!
> (Yes indeed!
> Yes, indeed!
> This is the battle-dance!

Behold my victor-weapon
And see this mighty blow,
And the foemen dead
That strew our battlefield!)

"And many another fierce war-song we chanted, and we feasted on the Fish-of-Whiro, and returned to Rotorua with our plunder and our captives."

The ancient warrior delighted to tell of those gloriously wild days of his youth. It was good to see that he was no Maori Chadband, hypocritically deprecating the excesses of the past. It was plain that those savage adventures were the best of his life. War was a supreme recreation of the Maori; and as for man-eating, why, it was all part of the great game.

He was well on to a century of years when he was found one day by his grandchildren sleeping the long sleep, as the poetic Maori phrase goes, in a warm bathing spring near his home at Owhatiura. The venerable warrior-sage's end was as deliciously peaceful as his youth was fierce and stormy.

So passed the last of the fighting Ngati-Tu. "Haere ra, Te Araki! Haere ra! (Farewell Te Araki! Farewell!)"

WEAPONS, WAR-DANCES

Probably the most handsome as well as the most effective weapon of wood ever invented by a warrior race is the Maori taiaha, specimens of which are so numerous in our museums. It is not merely a museum exhibit, either. It is one of the favourite symbols of old chieftainship handled at ceremonial gatherings. The orator has not quite lost the ancient art of taki-ing to and fro, in a measured space, sometimes breaking into a kind of trot, with now and again a little jump, as he delivers his speech, emphasising his words with gestures and taiaha-action. The greenstone mere and hardwood taiaha—they are perfect alike for close-quarters combat and for the conference on the marae under the shining sun, where a man must flourish something in his hand if he is to give animated and graceful point to his address.

A perfectly made and balanced taiaha, with its collar of red kaka feathers, is a beautiful weapon, combining the uses of a broadsword, quarter-staff, club and spear—a long, tapering, flattened shaft or blade, broadening towards the end, terminating at the other extremity in a tongue-shaped spearhead.

Akeake was the most favoured wood for the manufacture of the taiaha. I have handled some made of manuka, but they were rather heavy. I noted the great length of some of these two-handed weapons. Only a man of exceptional strength and height and length of arm could use them. They must have been handled by men quite 6 feet 6 inches in height. Such a man, active and expert in the handling of the taiaha, could sweep a whirlwind track through his foes, making terrific play with lightning-like blow and thrust. A good taiaha-wielder has proved more than a match for a swordsman. A mimic combat between two of the older school of Maoris, skilled in the use of the weapon, is an excellent exhibition of the fine art of fencing.

"Watch your opponent's toes," said a Maori when giving me some words of wisdom on the handling of the taiaha. He explained that it was necessary thus to anticipate a sudden blow, especially at the beginning of a duel, by observing the sudden down-pressure of the foot, and especially the big toe. Of course, the taiaha man did not wear boots. You had to dart glances everywhere in the deft play of this Maori substitute of the claymore.

Even in the wars when pakeha and Maori clashed, the old native weapons were not altogether discarded. The old men often carried their treasured greenstone clubs, for use at close-quarters; and some of the white colonial soldiers followed the example of the Maori fighter and carried a short-handled tomahawk at their waist-belts.

Some of the so-called war-dances as performed for the amusement of the pakeha nowadays are simply hakas, or action songs, rhythmic shouting with foot stamps and vigorous movements of the hands. A real war-dance is perhaps beyond their capacity today.

Memories come of some thrilling war-dances in the past, for example, the peruperu or tutu-waewae, performed with guns, by three hundred Waikato men at the mourning ceremonies over King Tawhiao at Taupiri, in 1894. Another, of a different character but greatly exciting, was a war-dance by the Taupo men at Rotorua in 1901 before the late King George V and Queen Mary (when Duke and Duchess of Cornwall and York). This peruperu, given by the Ngati-Tuwharetoa tribe, was the finest feature of the exhibition of tribal war-dances. The men's entry into the great marae, pursuing their tangata-wero or spear-thrower, was a spectacle of old-time revived.

As they halted in a compact company, or matua, 120 strong, in rank six warriors deep, their axe-shaped feather-plumed tewhatewhas raised high in the air, they looked a really formidable party. Then at the word from Te Heuheu, their fiery-eyed chief, who bounded lightly along the front ranks, the long narrow company, in battle array, sprang into ferocious attitudes and leaped this way and that, thrusting their weapons now one side, now the other, and with fierce grimaces and wild glaring eyes they roared out an ancient war-song.

They leaped like deer; again when they were off the ground they looked like some fierce horde of birds on the wing. As the song ended, the half-naked ranks, their painted faces turned on one side, with their weapons brandished, came down with a tremendous thud that made the earth shake.

7

THE LAW OF TAPU

Now and again comes a story which indicates that the ancient beliefs have not all been pressed out of the mental fabric of the Maori by the iron of the Pakeha. The faith in the law of tapu and the dread of makutu, or witchcraft, still linger, and are not likely to disappear for some time to come. The reverence for sacred things as embodied in the tapu rules of life is a salutary custom. These kura could consist of tribal heirlooms, one of the most sacred and famous of which was the serpentine bird, Korotangi (illustrated opposite) which is probably of Asiatic origin. Kura were kept in small carved treasure-houses, of which we see an example on page 41; they could also be natural features such as rocks or trees.

The real Maori does not care to discuss sacred matters in a place where food is being eaten; and an offshoot of this olden inhibition is the present-day practice of leaving pipe and tobacco outside a church before entering, tobacco being regarded as food.

The veneration of ancestors produces an intense regard for the last resting-places of the dead; and interference by Europeans with a Maori cemetery arouses the deepest indignation among the people whose forefathers' bones have been stolen. Not long ago Maoris would have enforced respect for the sacred places with their double-barrel guns.

An incident which occurred at Rotorua, illustrated the fear of infringing the mystic ban of tapu. An elderly woman of Ohinemutu, when walking over the ancient pa and burial place on Muruika Point, behind the Maori Church, thoughtlessly took a cigarette to smoke. Before she had time to light it she remembered that she was on tapu ground and refrained from smoking there, but she broke the cigarette and allowed some of the tobacco to fall on the ground.

This unintentional and trifling breach of the unwritten law brought serious consequences. When she left the sacred ground she smoked the portion of the cigarette she had kept, but her conscience was uneasy as she related afterwards. That night the retribution of the gods fell upon her. She felt a sudden pain shoot up her right arm, and she knew that her punishment had begun. In a little while the arm had swollen up to twice its ordinary size, and she was in agony.

It was no use calling in a pakeha doctor. She asked her family to send for her elder brother, who lived some miles away. He was a wise man, learned in the olden rites. He came and dealt with the case according to the manner of the tohunga, with the ancient recitals and magic touch. The relief was speedy; the woman's suffering was relieved, and her arm was soon down to its normal condition; her fears vanished. She had suffered her punishment; that offence had been expiated.

Who can explain the exact physical and mental processes which operate in such a case as this? We know a little of the influence of the mind over matter, but science has only touched the fringe of the problem. To the old Maoris, however, the inter-relation of the two incidents, the infringement of the tapu and the sudden illness in the night, is perfectly clear.

An old New Zealand settler told a story of his young days in Otago in illustration of the pawky particularity of Scottish folk about the Sabbath. When he was a boy, he was sent for a quart of milk on Sunday to a suburban farm kept by an old Scots body. He offered payment, and she said, "Weel, laddie, it's Sunday and I canna tak' your money, but pit it on the mantelshelf and I'll get it the morn's morn."

When I read that little story I remembered my old Ngati-Pikiao acquaintance Wineti, of Rotoiti, in the Rotorua Lakes Country. There was a famous and exceedingly tapu war canoe lying half-buried in the swampy ground at Tapuwae-haruru, close under the towering mountain range of Matawhaura. It had a tragic war story, and it was wont to be used as a funeral barge on the lake, taking the bodies of the dead to the feet of a steep track which led from the waterside to the great burial cavern of the tribe hundreds of feet above.

Wineti, one evening many years ago, showed me that mossy relic of the past. I examined it closely but my guide stood well off and exhibited relief when I joined him and we left the tapu spot. Thoughtlessly, when I joined him I offered him some tobacco as we walked away towards the village. Wineti wouldn't touch it. "No," he said, "not now and not here. But if you are still at Tapuwae-haruru I will take it tomorrow morning."

Herein Wineti and Mrs McSporran were brother and sister under their skins, in their respect for the conventions of tapu. In the Maori's case the feeling was deeper. He had a

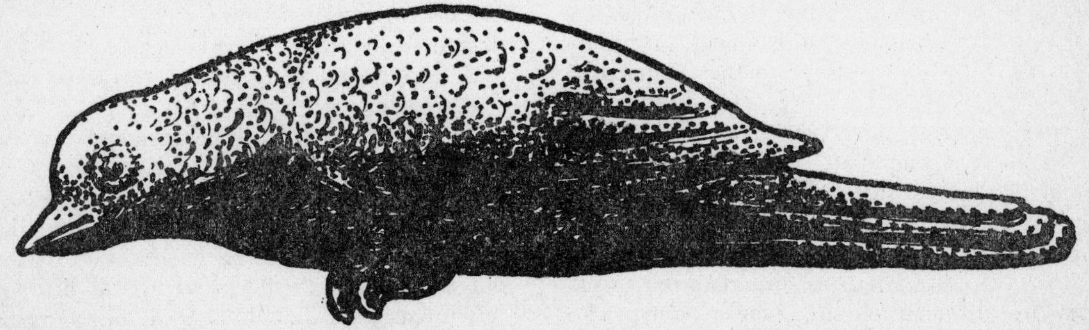

real dread of handling food and its like—tobacco is food to the Maori—within danger distance either in space or time of a tapu object.

The Belief in Witchcraft

Instances of the long-lingering Maori fear of the malignant exercise of occult arts by tohunga makutu, or tohunga whaiwhaia (wizards) still occasionally come to one's knowledge. The faith in makutu, or whaiwhaia, has perhaps been driven underground by modern education, but it is sometimes resurrected in an unexpected manner. Intertribal disputes, such as those over native titles, followed by deaths, have been frequent causes of accusation of witchcraft. The ancient ritualistic recitals for the removal of enemies by will power—killing by Maori wireless—are by no means forgotten. I had an excellent set of curses, of quite ferocious import, given to me by an old man of the King Country who affirmed their efficacy; he skilfully explained that they were only used for the purpose of killing wizards.

There are still very many Maori people who believe that men and women with uncanny powers practise their magic arts and possess the keys of life and death. I knew several men who, in their own belief and that of their people, are possessed of unusual psychic mana, and who are on occasion called upon to use their powers to combat the evil spells of others, to cure mysterious illnesses, which are soon diagnosed by them as due to makutu.

A certain old chief in the Arawa country was grievously concerned lately over the deaths in rapid succession of all his grandchildren. He and his friends attributed the visitation, otherwise inexplicable, to the evil magic spells and incantations of an enemy. They believed that the object of that jealous enemy was to wipe out the family, so that there would be none left to carry on the name. Some people, however, have used old fears to carry on a profitable calling in the name of healing the sick and afflicted. These cases are becoming more isolated as the years pass.

It is a very serious thing in Maoridom to accuse a person of practising the arts of makutu. It is no matter for ridicule. There have been actions for slander in the law courts over such accusations, and the evidence adduced has revealed the strength of the popular belief in occult arts.

There was a curious incident in a Maori Land Court on the East Coast in 1916, when formal complaint was laid that one of the parties had approached an old woman tohunga, otherwise a witch, with a request that she should influence the Court's judgment in favour of the applicant. The judge perceived that he could not ignore this, and he felt it necessary to reassure the people by telling them that they need have no fear of the tohunga's influence on the Court or themselves, and warning them to pay no attention to claims of supernatural powers.

There have been many more recent glimpses into the mental attitude of the Maori toward the cult of makutu. The young and educated generation may deride the mystery man's business, but events in the pakeha world frequently remind that even in this material, civilised age, old and primitive influences are strong. The layer-on of hands still plies his trade, the strong mentality commands the weaker; great is the power of suggestion.

The pakeha is not usually supposed to be subject to the Maori makutu or the Maori tapu. But to the Maori mind it is quite reasonable to suppose that pakeha powers of witchcraft exist. In a manuscript account of a Maori gathering of lamentation at Taupo, when the news of Sir Donald Maclean's death reached there, early in 1877, I found a suggestion of this. The old warrior chief Hauauru ("West Wind") of Ngati-Maniapoto, happened to be at Taupo at the time and he was one of the orators who

bewailed the untimely death of the Native Minister. "Perhaps", he said, addressing the spirit of 'Te Makarini', "you died so soon, in the midst of your work, because you were bewitched by some evil persons in Parliament who were jealous of your success in dealing with Maori matters."

8

THE LORE OF THE FOREST

WE WHO LIVE in a land of such glorious native forest—if we have any poetry or imagination at all—cannot but enter in some degree into the feeling of reverence with which the ancients regarded the forest primeval. Primitive people looked with intense respect on the great green kings of the woods, those solemn pillars which had seen so many generations of men live their little lives and pass away. The nature-worship which was man's earliest religion centred to a considerable extent around remarkable trees, mountains and rocks, and here in New Zealand, as in ancient Greece, in the oak groves of Britain, or in the Black Forest in Germany, the grand growths of the deep woodlands were often objects to be approached with ceremonial care and reverential feeling. The vast and gloomy woods exercise an overpowering awe. The natives of Siberia call their thousand-mile stretches of pine and larch forests "places where the mind is lost".

The Maori enshrined deities and sprites and fairy beings in the noble trees of that woodland which was to him so full of mystery. The shadowy deeps of the bush, the tall silent columns, like chieftains, with their heads in the sky, the sudden sharp cries of the hidden birds, and the damp cool fragrance which steeped everything, impressed primitive man profoundly. The simple mind saw sentient beings in certain trees; dryads and spirits haunted the dark shadowy glades and gullies and shadowy ridges, and peeped from behind the wide-spreading buttresses. The ancient forest-explorer was in an enchanted land. Emerson, in one of his essays, quotes a friend as saying that the woods always seemed to her to wait, as if the genii which inhabited them suspended their deeds till the wayfarer had passed on. This is much the same idea as that which possessed the minds of the Polynesians who peopled this country. Uncanny folk, fairies, the patupaiarehe, turehu, heketoro, and maero, lurked in the heart of the forest.

The pakeha's regard for New Zealand's indigenous trees is chiefly based on considerations of unusual size and beauty. The Maori, having been here much longer, has had time to build poetic and romantic associations about many a tree. The tendency of all primitive peoples to invest forests with mystery and supernatural attributes was particularly marked in Maori-dom. To this day certain trees are identified with the memories of celebrated ancestors. The sacred matai (black pine) tree, called Hine-hopu on Hongi's Track, between Lakes Rotoiti and Rotoehu, the present main highway from Rotorua to Whakatane on the East Coast—is an example. The custom which many travellers observe of laying offerings of leaves at the hollow foot of the ancient tree is a practice observed in several other countries.

Another tapu tree is a beautiful totara on Mokoia Island, Rotorua. There are trees with sacred associations and attributes in the Urewera Country and along the Bay of Plenty coast, in North Auckland, at Kawhia, and other places along the West Coast, in the King Country, and indeed all over the Maori-peopled parts of the North Island. No legislation, no Order-in-Council or Departmental interdict is required to protect them from Maori hands. The knowledge of their history is enough.

There have been exceptions, when enemies have destroyed trees tapu to the local tribe, or have deliberately flouted the tapu's spell in order to provoke a conflict. Now and again a man imbued with pakeha notions has scoffed at the tapu and done violence alike to sacred tree and popular beliefs, sometimes with unfortunate results to himself.

THE BIRD-HUNTER'S METHODS

Contrast old-time Maori ways of taking birds in bush, swamp, river and lake with the popular gunning pastime of today. The Maori killed wild fowl in great numbers. He observed close seasons, and when the bird-hunting time came the whole community took part in it. It was true sport, in the sense that the hunters enjoyed it greatly and yet did not heedlessly

kill birds or waste the game taken. The hunting was strictly for the pot, or rather the hangi or umu, the earth oven. The Maori did not kill birds for the mere sport of the thing, for the sake of exhibiting his skill in slaughter. The pigeon, kaka, tui, and other bush birds which were in vast numbers in the bush, and the grey duck (parera) formed a very large part of the native sources of food supply, and the process of capturing and preserving the birds of the forest and swamps and waters was an important industry of the Maori life.

Centuries of existence and food-quest in these islands had produced a vast store of bush lore, and many ingenious methods of

still families who allow their womenfolk to eat certain parts only of the birds that are caught. When I was first in the Urewera Country, in 1898, the long slender spears were still being used in the Ruatahuna and Maungapohatu districts. These 25-foot and 30-foot spears were the product of long and patient industry, for they were cut out and gradually fined down from a tawa tree. A great many mutu-kaka, the snaring apparatus with which the last bush parrot was caught, were also seen in the villages; they were taken out and set in position, chiefly in the tops of rata trees, when the season for fowling came round, when the birds were in best condition from feeding on the forest fruits and the nectar of the rata.

The mutu-kaka was a kind of perch cut from a forked branch, and rigged with a running tackle and a noose contrivance which caught the kaka by the legs just above the claws when it settled on the perch, which was made fast to the end of a pole and pushed up to the top of the tree. The hunter, with the end of the flax line in his hand, sat in the branches below, or sometimes on the ground, until a kaka was caught by the quick twitch of the rope. Then he belayed the tackle and climbed quickly, or drew down the pole to which the perch was fastened, and killed the bird by biting it at the back of the head, then arranged his tackle for the next bird.

Long spears, tipped with bone or iron barbs, with which the pigeon or tui were killed, were to be seen hung along the walls in the large meeting-houses at Ruatahuna and elsewhere in the Urewera Country in the off season. They were too long to be stored in any ordinary whare. Sometimes the hunter would not go to the trouble of taking his spear home, but would leave it suspended from a tree. Being so long and slender, not more than an inch in thickness, it was not an easy weapon to handle in the bush. The hunter usually carried it trailing behind him, holding it near the barbed point.

An old mountaineer and bushman who showed me how to use it, near Mataatua one day, was an expert in this, and all other branches of bushcraft. With the utmost care, making not a sound or disturbing a twig or

obtaining the feathered harvest of the forest. The principal means used before the pakeha shotgun was introduced were long spears and various kinds of snares, and even to modern times these primitive and effective devices remained in use in some Maori tribal districts, because not only were they cheaper than guns and ammunition but they did not frighten away the birds. The Maori found that shooting had the effect in the long run of driving the pigeon, kaka, tui and duck to other districts, whereas spearing and snaring could not appreciably affect the abundance of bush game.

In some parts of the King Country—chiefly the Hurakia-Tuhua Ranges, in West Taupo, the Upper Wanganui, and South Kawhia—and in the Urewera Country, the old foresters' ways persisted long after they had been abandoned elsewhere. Even today, the Urewera people observe some old customs. It is considered bad luck to pluck a bird in the bush and there are leaf, he pushed the thin spear up through the branches, keeping it close to the trunk of the tree, until with a sudden dexterous thrust he impaled his bird in the breast. That spear, like most of the other apparatus for fowling on which so much skill and ingenuity and labour were expended, has probably by this time been annexed by some museum. A shorter spear (tao) was used by tree-climbers or by those who hunted in places where pigeon were to be found on low branches.

Snares were set over a wooden drinking trough which was placed on a suitable branch when the berries were ripe, the birds became more thirsty and flew to the troughs for water, where they were ensnared as their heads went through the loops to reach the water.

Such were some of the bush-hunting ways of the past. The convenient method of the pac is still used on occasions in the Urewera. This is a rough shelter of ferntree fronds erected in a place where kaka parrots abound. It is just large enough to shelter the bird-hunter. He imitates the screech call of the kaka, which comes fluttering about in its inquisitive way, and is knocked over with a stick. The kaka is still seen and heard in large numbers in the Urewera bush; sometimes it deserts one part for another for a season or two in its quest for food. A decoy kaka (mokai) was often used. Every village had its captive kaka, which was taken out and made fast by the leg, and the hunter taught it to utter its screeches to attract its wild brethren of the bush to the fern-frond screen where its owner crouched on watch.

Turning to the capture of water-fowl, there is the chase of the grey duck (parera). Hunting the duck with dogs was a widely observed method; the duck-chase was carried out at moulting-time, when the margins of the swamps and lagoons were the scenes of capture. There were other methods, one of which was the practice of swimming slowly and silently, the hunter's head encircled with rushes and tufts of flax, until a flock of ducks was approached, and then deftly pulling one under water, killing it and attaching it to the waist-belt, then repeating the procedure. By a cautious approach of this kind, floating almost imperceptibly up to the ducks, the disguise seeming a drifting tuft of rushes, a skilful hunter could take bird after bird. This was a practice on the lakes and lagoons. The Ngati-Pikiao, of Rotoiti and thereabouts, for example, had a favourite duck-hunting water, the arm of Lake Rotoehu, which the present motor road skirts near Hongi's Track.

Still another method, and the one chiefly used, was to arrange snares, in the form of loops of running nooses, of flax or cabbage tree leaf in the narrow channels and runways among the sedge and rushes and raupo in the swamps

and on the lake margins. Often the growing rushes were tied together over the little channels in loops, close to the water, in such a way that duck, teal or other waterfowl swimming along there would be caught by the neck. The birds' struggles when entangled in these meshes only drew the loops tighter. In some places, such as the great Ngaere Swamp in Taranaki, near Stratford, the kotuku, or white heron, was at one time plentiful and it, too, was often caught in snares.

In North Auckland, the shallow Lake Tangonge, in the Kaitaia district, was the scene of duck hunts on a great scale in former times. The Maoris dug a canal from the lake to tidal waters for the capture of both duck and eels. The former they took in large numbers by means of flax nets stretched across the wide ditch from bank to bank. The hunters in canoes, by slow and gradual closing in, worked the unsuspecting parera from the lake towards the mouth of the canal and then when they had them there drove them along to the net. Too late the closely-crowded flock of duck rose to fly and encountered the nets of the hundred loops. In this way great numbers of parera were taken every season.

Whether in the forest, swamp, lake or river, the Maori's ways of capturing his feathered game were the product of many generations of experience and close study of bird habit. And his bird-hunting, though yielding him a continual, generous supply of food, did not diminish the bird-stock. All kinds of birds teemed in bush and lake, and would be teeming there today had not the pakeha revolutionised the ways of slaughter and imported enemies of the native birds. Whenever the numbers of birds in a hunting ground showed a decrease, a protective rahui was proclaimed and there was serious trouble ahead for any greedy person who disregarded the close season.

The Maori were very particular in their observance of the ceremonial customs pertaining to the chase of the birds, the life of Tane-Mahuta's ancient forests. There were mauri, usually stones, which had been made tapu by the tohungas and which were placed in some spot in the forest to preserve the life of the bush, and ensure a permanent supply of birds for the sustenance of the owners. The opening of the snaring and spearing seasons was observed with ritual, and the first birds taken were laid at the sacred place as an offering to the deities of the forest. Every bush-owning community has these places of the first-fruits. The late Rangiriri, the last tohunga of his clan of the Arawa, showed me the tapu spot, in a fern-hung shallow grotto cut out of the cliff at Tihi-o-Tonga bush, where the first birds killed each season were laid as an offering to Tane. This place is about five miles from Rotorua Town.

9

ARTCRAFT OF THE MAORI

THE RICHLY CARVED and brightly painted meeting-house, the carved war-canoe, and the elaborate moko or tattoo on face and body were the principal forms in which the native genius for artcraft and decoration found eye-pleasing display. The Maori artisan was also an artist. He combined utility with decoration as probably no other primitive race combined them. Whenever it was possible with his carving chisel he wrought spirals and gargoyles and chevrons on the wood he worked, preferably the durable and easily cut totara. Weapons, paddle-handles, canoe-balers, bird-snare perches, all were carved more or less. But it was in the house slabs and frontal barge boards and in the canoe figureheads and stern-posts that he excelled.

Maori architecture was evolved by centuries of life in this country. It adds to, not detracts from the attraction of the landscape. Fortunately the cheap and horrible pakeha shack is gradually disappearing in Maori villages as better homes are built in their place. But there is a distinct revival of the carving art and the ancient form and colour scheme. Nearly every village of importance now has one or more carved houses built in the old-fashioned style. Maori architecture has undergone many changes with the introduction of new building materials which have made maintenance easier.

Modern carved houses are better ventilated, have better lighting and domestic facilities compared with the older type.

In the revival of the wood-carving art a small industry of great interest was established. Before the commencement of the Maori Arts Board's operations, there was every indication that the carver's art would be lost to New Zealand, as there were but few of the old carvers left, and since the school was started these have died. There were several student carvers who are employed by the board, and under the direction of Mr H. Hamilton, they made splendid progress. All the carvings done at the school were a true representation of the Maori art, and were based on correct designs and copies of ancient carvings. Outstanding carvers still find employment decorating new carved houses with all the beauty of an ancient art done with modern methods in changed conditions.

The artistic side of the Maori is exhibited, too, in the robes and cloaks, popularly and inadequately described as mats, in the weaving and decorating of which very great care was expended. These flax and feather garments represented an art in fabrics considerably in advance of that of some of the Polynesians. The feather cloaks of the people, worn on festive occasions over their ordinary clothes, are brilliant in their variety of colour and pattern. Some are short capes just covering the shoulders; others fall in a graceful drape from the neck to the feet. In some of the feather garments the outer side is composed of the brown feathers of the kiwi (Apteryx) stitched into the flaxen material. There are handsome cloaks and robes covered with rows of pigeon, tui, kaka parrot, and even peacock's feathers, the iridescent blues and yellows and reds gleaming rainbow-like.

There are preserved in museums many garments covered with soft white tufts of hair of the now-extinct Maori dog. The cloak most often seen is the korowai, a finely dressed fabric of soft white flax, ornamented with dangling thrums of black-dyed flax.

The head-dresses, worn on special occasions, are very decorative, though they may consist only of one or two of the white-tipped tail-feathers of the huia, a feather of the long-tailed cuckoo, or white goose-feathers. Coronet-like chaplets of diamond-patterned coloured flax or of brown kiwi feathers are worn by many at tribal gatherings.

It is the custom among many speakers and writers dealing with the subject of Maori art in wood-carving and other forms to assign remote foreign origins to many of the patterns and designs. For the bases of the curvilinear forms which are the most prominent in carving and painting in Maori decorated houses they go to Asiatic and other sources, and find even in North European primitive art the concepts which could be the original inspiration of our native New Zealand woodwork design. One lecturer mentioned the close resemblance between scrolls carved on ancient monumental stones in Ireland and the double spirals in the prow of a Maori war canoe, and referred to the likeness between certain other Maori carvings and emblems in Assyrian and Hindu mythological art. Other authorities have cited sculptured figures and symbols in many parts of the world, such as Cambodia and Mexico, and have built thereon a structure of derivations designed to show that the Maori simply perpetuated here art motive which he had brought with him in his long migrations from the older-peopled countries.

I am disposed to take the opposite view, and to offer the suggestion that the Maori derived his chief inspiration from his peculiar New Zealand environment, and that the resemblance between his carving and tattoo patterns and other forms of artcraft and the sculpture and carving of far-distant lands are in the nature of coincident developments of art such as might be expected to arise in any country inhabited by a people given to close observation of natural objects.

The spiral design in particular is one which, in every part of the world, is exhibited in primitive or semi-primitive art. It is the Maori who has brought it to perfection, his pitau pattern which enters so largely into every branch of artistry.

Superficial likenesses have often led students, as well as casual observers, into linking up the Maori-Polynesian with the Old World peoples.

Undoubtedly certain links exist, as in language, religion and customs. But it seems to me to overstrain the probabilities to assert an Asiatic basis for carving, and to declare, as in one book, that the Maori probably derived his tattoo patterns and his style of fortification from Melanesian sources. It does not seem reasonable to deny originality of idea to the Maori and to overlook the possibility that he found his principal inspiration in these islands of ours, with their great land masses—after the circumscribed tropic isles of the Pacific—their vast forests of tall timber, their wealth of ferns and wild flowers, and the innumerable aspects of beauty in Nature and human life which would inevitably impress the eye and soul of an art-craftsman.

It must be remembered that the islands of New Zealand were first colonised by Polynesians probably a thousand years ago, and that such a period would give abundant time in which such a race could evolve arts and industries entirely on their own. In clothing, in buildings, in canoes and fortifications the Maori certainly displayed an originality and skill born of long centuries of effort in adapting the natural resources of the country to his needs. Similarly, in art designs, he may be conceded the credit of having evolved the most characteristic forms of decorations from his surroundings and life after arrival on these shores from the Eastern Pacific. There is no need, say some present day scholars, to bring in any outside influences to explain the origin and development of Maori art.

The pitau, or spiral, which the Maori carver and tattooer used and elaborated could have been derived from many sources independently of such origins as the snaky coil of Asia and Europe and America. The coiled serpent, "type of the endless and unknown", is seen alike on ancient Aztec temples and on Celtic memorials. But the coil of a rope might easily suggest itself as a like pattern to the artist's eye, just as the shape of the bishop's crozier may have been suggested to our European forefathers by the curling shoots of a fern. Indeed, old Maori carvers, the artcraftsmen of the past generations, have told me that the pitau was derived from the young closely-curled fronds of the tree

fern. Again, a carver turned up his thumb and said "Observe these fine close curved lines—are they not like the pitau I am carving here?"

Yet again, as that most gifted of all the Arawa carvers, the venerable Anaha, once reminded me, the web of a spider (wharepungawerewere) is exactly a spiral; and this indeed is the motif, complete to its connecting or supporting lines radiating from the centre, which is copied in the openwork designs of the war-canoe figurehead.

Other sources and suggestions have been indicated to me by the skilled artists of various tribes. There is a celebrated white sandstone cliff called Otamahuka, on the Bay of Plenty coast near Matata, where the vertical face has been weathered into a variety of curious forms. Spirals are there, and gargoyles and all manner of grotesque faces in relief; and the driving sand in gales from time to time wears new figures in the rock. There was a tattooing artist and carver long ago, Tamahuka, after whom the cliff of pictures was named; he studied the rock-face, says tradition, and obtained therefrom some of the inspiration for his fine chisel-work.

In other art-forms, such as the black and red rafter patterns, the original motif was taken from nature. The curl of wave is there, the drooping blossom of the kowhai, the curve of a cumulus cloud, the volute of a shell.

The carved marakihau, a kind of sea-god, seen in Bay of Plenty and Urewera meeting-houses, is, too, a local concept, peculiar to New Zealand. The source of the manaia, that strange figure with a bird-like beak, is more obscure. Some writers have tried to link it up with Melanesian designs. I think, however, that is originated in New Zealand, and is based on an artistic distortion of the human figure, like European gargoyles.

I have seen it suggested that the Maori borrowed his moko or tattoo patterns from the Melanesians, and also some of his carvings. He had no need to go to such a source; and most of the Melanesians did not tattoo like the Maoris. Nor did the Maori bring the moko we know with him from Polynesia. The face tattoo of the warriors, as well as the kauwae, or chin and lips tattoo of the women, was purely of New Zealand origin and development. The ancient tattoo of Polynesia was very different, rectilinear, as opposed to the Maori curvilinear. We read of that Eastern Pacific tattoo in Herman Melville's *Typee*. He described the warrior who looked out from behind bars, his straight-lined face-mask.

Down at Moeraki, on the North Otago coast, 30 years ago, I saw the very last relics of this Tahiti-Marquesas design of moko. There were two old men there, Ira Herewini and Wi Pokuku, whose faces bore horizontal blue lines, across nose and cheeks. There were two straight lines across Ira's face and one on Pokuku's crossing from ear to ear. They were the last men tattooed with the moko-a-Tamatea, which the old people explained was the pattern used by the chief who commanded the canoe *Takitimu,* one of the ancestral sailing craft from Tahiti. Tamatea was a skilled tattoo artist, and he and some of his crew settled awhile at the south end of Lake Te Anau, after he finally landed in Southland, and there he tattooed a number of his young men after the manner of the tropic homeland, with many lines across the face; and this moko was used for more than five hundred years, down to Herewini's and Pokuku's day.

A most curious survival, that old, old straightline tattoo. But the descendants of Tamatea and of the other canoe crews in course of time devised a far more artistic and intricate system of face-adornment, the pinnacle of indigenous artistry.

Much ceremony and sacred ritual were attendant on the opening of a newly-built carved house (whare-whakairo). The spell of tapu, which lay on the figures and parts of the building, the tapu of the forest-god, had to be laid by the priests with chant and prayer. It was usual also to place an offering beneath the house to propitiate the gods. The Maori had the custom of luck offerings developed to a high degree. No carved house was deemed safe unless a block of greenstone or some other treasure was laid in the hole in which the central house pillar, the poutokomanawa, was set up, to support the ridge pole. In olden days it was sometimes a slave instead of green-stone.

There are instances, too, of war parties having been sent out to slay some suitable victim for the offering to the spirit of the soil; and a victim also was killed to celebrate the launching of a new war canoe. Ancient and modern touch hands here in this atua-propitiation rite. The pakeha has his luck offerings. An example is the custom which prevailed in the U.S.A., when a race for the America Cup was impending, of depositing a twenty-dollar gold piece under the butt of the defending yacht's mast. Many other big racing craft had this lucky coin put there under the mast just before it was stepped.

It is a very ancient custom, this placing of a fortune-bringing emblem at the butt of the mast, usually the mainmast in a three- or two-masted vessel; as ancient as the practice of placing coins and other articles under the foundation stone of an important building. The idea is the far-back belief in universal magic and in the multitude of spirits, good and evil, which it was necessary to propitiate. The gold coin under the yacht's mast, or the mast of a prosaic trading vessel, for that matter, is a relic of an era when offerings were made to Neptune or Poseidon; to our Maori-Polynesians he is Tangaroa, the God of the Ocean and all that pertains thereto. In the case of buildings it is the olden offer of treasure to appease the deity, or demon, of the earth. So our church builders and layers of foundation stones in setting their coins are simply imitating the immemorial pagan custom.

10

THE WAR CANOE

THE MAORI greatly developed the science and art of canoe-making in this country of large and readily-worked timbers, in particular that valuable tree the totara. The many rivers, streams and lakes of the much-indented coast and its gulfs strewn with islands made the canoe an indispensable means of travel. Canoe-making became an important branch of native art-craftmanship, and upon the large waka-taua or war canoe was lavished the most careful and elaborate finish and decorations. A well-built waka-taua is an object of grace and beauty combined with strength and perfect fitness for its purpose.

Nowadays few new canoes are made, and the only surviving specimens of large waka-taua are in the museums with the solitary exception of a certain kauri canoe of great size and some history, the *Taheretikitiki,* which when last I saw it was hauled up, neglected, on an island in the Lower Waikato. A large true war-canoe in good condition still preserved is a handsome totara-built craft in the Auckland War Memorial Museum, the *Toki-a-Tapiri,* which is 82 feet in length, with a beam amidships of six feet.

About the year 1940, several new canoes were made in the Waikato under the stimulus of Princess Te Puea, who encouraged the few remaining craftsmen to instruct younger men in the ancient craft. Today, there is a small fleet of canoes at Ngaruawahia which can still be seen on ceremonial occasions.

With modern means of transit, in such places as the Waikato and the Wanganui, where river-canoeing was once universal, the pretty sight of an old-time craft, long, narrow and graceful, is becoming comparatively rare. A recent gathering on the Wanganui River saw the last twelve or so river canoes drawn up together on the bank. Some had topstrakes added and there was even one fitted with an outboard motor. However, the fine sport of canoe-racing will do something to keep the ancient art from dying out. On Rotorua Lake in former days the spectacle of large canoes under sail was a frequent characteristic picture of lakeland life. I have seen a small flotilla of canoes coming in to Ohinemutu together from Mokoia Island and Te Ngae with sprit-sails set before a favouring breeze; the wakas were loaded with produce from the native cultivations. Now the convenient motor launch has superseded the picturesque old dug-outs on most of our lakes and rivers. At one or two places, such as Horowhenua and Wairoa, there are dug-out canoes still to be seen in lakes and lagoons.

Canoe-racing is an often thrilling sport of the Maoris on the Waikato River, where aquatic sports gatherings are held annually. An amusing feature of such a regatta is the canoe hurdle-racing, in which small light canoes, each

carrying two, are impelled over hurdles about thirty inches above the surface of the water. Capsizes are frequent, but the canoe men and women are like ducks in the water.

Of a sterner character were the war-canoe races. In the days of the past one has seen many such exciting contests on the Lower Waikato River. I shall describe here a scene on the river, a particularly well-fought race at Mercer, where there is a splendid broad reach of water.

The contesting canoes were the *Paparata,* a kahikatea (white pine) log dug-out 80 feet in length, and and the *Whawhakia,* 75 feet. The *Paparata* carried forty-three paddlers, most of them kneeling two abreast; the other, a considerably lighter craft, was manned by a crew of twenty-eight, all picked canoeists. Amidships in each craft stood a hautuwaka, or fugleman, shawl-kilted, his head decked with white feathers and brandishing a whalebone club. Te Katipa was the hautu, giving the times to his men. The long canoes swept by in mid-stream going up to the starting-point. The grey old chief with a wave of his whalebone mere shouted to his crew: "Aue! Taringa whaka-rongo (O ears! Listen)"—This was by way of preparatory word or caution. Then he yelled the orders, "Hikitia (Lift up)" and "Pakia (Slap it)", whereupon every man raised his paddle clear above the canoe-side, missing one stroke, and with the other hand smartly slapped the dripping blade. The next moment each boatman once more dipped his paddle deep, and the canoes swept on along the shining waterway to the starting line.

At the starter's rifle-shot *Paparata* and *Whawhakia* got away well together. The course for the race was a distance of two miles with two turns. The seventy manuka paddles of the rival tribesmen dipped with the precision of a steam-engine as the long narrow craft shot up to the mark half a mile up the river, and the men at the steering paddles strained all their energies to secure the advantage in the sharp turn. The big *Paparata* was the first to turn, gaining nearly half a length at this point, and then down the wide smooth river they raced. With the paddles dipping all together, and the canoes shooting on under the mighty impulse

of the strong-armed crews the wakas resembled to the fancy two great winged water-reptiles.

Away down the current they dashed, the rows of paddles rising and falling like wet pinions, the canoes sweeping along at a great rate side by side, aided by the swift-flowing Waikato, the shoulders of the paddlers rising and bowing again in perfectly-drilled unison. Amidships in each canoe the captains balanced with the ease and grace of long practice, flourishing their weapons in measured time, and encouraging their men with voice and hands, and now and again bursting into short sharp chants. The *Paparata* put on a great spurt passing the crowd of spectators on the bank, and edged her rival near the wooded island. Very little change took place from this on the run to the lower turning-flag, three-quarters of a mile downstream, and we watched with growing excitement the flashing of the three-score and ten paddles in the sun as the sharp blades glistened for a moment and dipped again.

At the turning-mark, midway between the willow-shaded banks, the canoes rounded the flag almost together; and then commenced a beautiful race home. The *Whawhakia* steadily crept up, her crew working as for their lives, instead of for a few pounds' prize money. The frenzied captains were back in the days of old Maoriland. They waved their weapons and quivered their hands, now on this side, now on that, and grey old Katipa was in his element. His white whalebone club glinting in the sun, the old fugleman of the *Paparata* loudly chanted an ancient canoe-lilt of Waikato.

Every nerve is strained for victory, every pound is put on. The *Paparata's* bows are only a few yards ahead of her rival. The paddle-strokes come quicker and quicker, the captains furiously urge on their panting crews with

hoarse cries of "Hukere, hukere, Waikato!" "Tena tiaia!" and "Hoea, hoea! (Paddle away!)"

The spectators are frantic with excitement. Steadily, inch by inch, the *Whawhakia* crawls up on her opponent, but she cannot reach her bows. Paddling madly, the crews surge up to the finishing mark. Victory is *Paparata's* when the gun fires—but only by a fathom's length.

In the days of the past many a great canoe race has been seen on Auckland Harbour. In some of these a beautiful war-canoe of kauri, the *Taheretikitiki* now on the Waikato River, was engaged. In one notable race this waka defeated two naval cutters, manned by well-trained crews from H.M.S. *Tauranga*. The course was a mile and a half in length.

The *Taheretikitiki* made a brave show, decorated at the bow with a carved scrollwork figurehead, and at the stern with a high stern-post, at the foot of which was carved a tiki or human image. The stern was decorated with flax ornamental work, and from the front of the figurehead projected two long waving wands, known as puhi, like the antennae of the butterfly in shape, and adorned with bunches of albatross feathers. The canoe had a Waikato crew consisting of 53 men. Of these, 50 were the body of paddlers, kneeling two abreast. There were two steering paddles. Amidships stood the old warrior Te Paki. Nearly all the paddlers were stripped to the waist, while the rest wore singlets, and the men wore handkerchiefs bound round their brows and feathers in their hair.

The two man-of-war crews in their light cutters got well under way first, but the canoe soon gathered momentum, and was quickly speeding down the harbour, her fifty paddles dipping as one. Rounding their respective buoys, the two cutters got round more smartly than the *Taheretikitiki,* which took longer to turn owing to her great length, 84 feet. On the race from here up the Maori paddlers bent well to their work, but owing to a misunderstanding made a long sweep out of the direct line in order to round a certain mark-boat for yachts. This made her course several hundreds of yards longer than was necessary, and the *Tauranga's* first crew passed her as if the canoe had been standing still. However, the plucky canoeists were not daunted. Urged on by the frantic shouts of Te Paki, balancing himself amidships, the paddlers redoubled their efforts. The *Taheretikitiki* made a splendid turn at the up-harbour mark, taking a beautiful sweep, and came round as if on a pivot for the last half mile.

Now, Te Paki's voice was raised in fierce yells to his canoeists, and his whalebone club circled round and quivered quicker than ever. Waikato must beat the sailor men whatever comes. Faster and faster dipped the paddles, the great canoe surged along between lines of foam. Before half the distance homeward was covered the Waikato men had caught the first cutter by dint of the hardest paddling, and fairly ran away from the bluejackets. Cheered by the roars of applause from the shore they bent still harder to their work and passed the winning post a length ahead of the *Tauranga's* first crew. The other naval cutter was several lengths behind when she finished. And a triumphant, vociferous haka by the Maori spectators greeted the weary but joyful victors as they drew into the beach.

Interesting links with the past are seen in the supposed anchor stones of famous canoes. In the Dominion Museum there is the anchor stone of Kupe's canoe, while in the New Plymouth Museum the *Tokomaru's* is on display. Near Mokau an imitation concrete canoe is the base for the *Tainui's* anchor stone, a measure adopted to prevent a repetition of its removal, as had happened previously.

11

THE TANGI

ONG AND ELOQUENT ELEGIES, couched in language often highly figurative and sometimes curiously archaic, are heard at many a Maori tangihanga, the mourning ceremony over the dead of the tribe. Ancient poems are brought in and adapted to the needs of the moment by the mourning orators. Chants composed in the traditional Hawaiki before the historical sailing canoes crossed the ocean to New Zealand are remembered today. The slow monotone in which they are sung sometimes acts as a soporific; at any rate, that has been my experience.

But there is one funeral chant that is not droned out in slow time. Fierce, indignant, vociferous, it is an expression of horror at a tribal calamity. It is the shortest dirge I know, but into its few words there is compressed much meaning. Only under very special circumstances is it sung.

It was at the seafront village at Matata, on the Bay of Plenty coast, in January, 1919, when every Maori tribe, like every pakeha community, was mourning the terrible ravages of the influenza plague. A friend and I were staying at the one hotel in the township, when we received a message from the heads of the local Maori people, the Tawera and Ngati-Rangitihi, clans of the Arawa, inviting us to visit their kainga for the ceremony of mourning over the losses in the epidemic. In Matata and its near settlements forty people had died in a few weeks.

The invitation was in compliment to my old friend, a captain in the New Zealand forces and a New Zealand Cross man, who had been associated with these people for nearly fifty years and had led them on the warpath against Te Kooti in the last Hauhau wars. Rather remarkable, too, was the fact that the local folk and many visitors from other tribes were holding a tangi over Te Nia, one of Te Kooti's numerous widows, who had just died.

It was a place of sights and sounds to thrill the onlookers. We stood for nearly an hour on the marae facing the carved meeting-house "Rangiaohia" while the orators addressed my veteran companion and bewailed the tragedy which had come to the tribe, his tribe. Groups of people sat about the sides of the wide, grassy assembly ground, and there was a compact body of mourners in front of the porch of "Rangiaohia" where the warrior woman who had seen so much of wild adventure with her savage chief lay in state, her hair dressed with white feathers, the finest of cloaks laid over her. On a tall flagstaff flew at half-mast a bright banner inscribed with the ancestral name Te Apumoana.

There was a never-ceasing background of lamentation, the steady hum of grief, the rise and fall of the women's wail, like the sound of surf on the coast, now and again a high cry like a seagull's. The green marae slanted gently to the Awa-a-te-Atua waters, and out beyond there were the sandhills and surf-edged blue of ocean; the black Rurima Rocks protruded from the sparkling sea like the teeth of mako sharks; and on the sea-line far away a high, rounded mass of steam made a nimbus of yellow and white above the sulphur volcano of Whakaari, White Island.

The orators compared the influenza disaster to the destruction of their people in the Tarawera eruption of 1886. It was Moura over again—Moura of tragic memory, the village on Lake Tarawera's shore where forty of Ngati-Rangitihi were overwhelmed and entombed forever in the muddy ash hurled from the volcano and from Lake Rotomahana. They pictured the long-dead of the tribe assembling in the spiritland to greet their many grandchildren, as they entered the sad gates of the Reinga. It was like a battlefield, so many were the dead. Presently, they said, we will take you to see their resting place and they will hear the near reverberations of your footsteps as you tread the ground above them.

A literal translation would not convey anything like the effect intended and embodied in those lines. The mourner sang his abhorrence of the evil death which had befallen his people, "death of a serf, a slave". Had they but fallen in battle, at the hands of warriors, it would have been a death of glory. "Your heads would have been adorned with the plumes of the albatross, the ocean would have been paddled over by war-canoe crews seeking to avenge your deaths."

Hapimana's delivery of the sharp staccato chant was intentionally harsh, discordant. It expressed the mourners' hatred of a miserable death, disgust at such a stroke of Fate. In Alfred Domett's *Ranolf and Amohia* there is a long and eloquent paraphrase of this ancient "Matekino" dirge. Domett took this theme and expanded it into a chant of thrill and fine imagery. He pictured the avengers' war canoes —had it been a warrior's fitting death—darting all together, forward through the foam together:

"Fierce deep cries the paddles timing,
  While the paddles' serried rows,
  Like broad birds' wings spread and close."

The head man of the kainga presently took us to the tribal burial place on a neighbouring

Then at one side of the marae, rose up a black-bearded man, the chief, Pohonui Hapimana. Without any oratorical preamble, he chanted in a great harsh voice, tremendously strong and rough, these words:

"Mate kino, mate kino,
Mate taurekareka!
Me he taua pea
Koe i mate ai,
E tataia ki te toroa,
E hoea i te moana!"

mound, and showed us where the lately dead were laid. The rows of graves were all completely covered with small white shells, beautifully arranged, shells gathered from the ocean beach, the loving work of the sorely grieving ones. There was a north-east breeze blowing, and the voice of the surf mingled with the cadence of the tangi that came from the bowed groups of women in front of the meeting-house below us. A long wisp of vapour from the gleaming sulphur cumulus that clung to White Island trended landward, drifted towards the Awa-a-te-Atua.

"See", said Hapimana, "Whakaari is mourning too; the volcano god is sending us his message of love and sorrow."

12

AMUSEMENTS OF THE MAORI

ACTIVE and vigorous and athletic, the old-time Maori found his, and her, greatest diversion in village life in the dance in its various forms. Both sexes could take part in the haka, in which rhythmic shouting and chanting were emphasised with stamp of foot and actions of the hands. The poi, action-song rather than dance, is the performance of the women and girls, and very pretty and captivating it is, with its grace of action, its swing and tap of raupo-reed balls in perfect time, and its haunting melodies.

Unfortunately, the trail of pakeha manners is over the action-song nowadays, except in such districts as Taranaki, where the people are more conservative than in most other parts.

Visitors to Rotorua enjoy as one of the special attractions of that wonderful region the dance-and-song entertainments given by the sweet singers and expert poi-parties of Ohinemutu and Whakarewarewa. There, however, as at Otaki and elsewhere, pakeha tunes and instruments have been introduced. But the real old-time poi is that of some of the Taranaki people who adhere to the ways of the past as taught by their venerated leader Te Whiti, the prophet of Parihaka.

There the poi is a kind of patriotic and religious ritual as well as an entertainment. The women and girls wear in their hair the raukura, the patriotic symbol, consisting of white feathers, which toss and wave in the motions of the dance, and their cheeks are marked with black and red war-paint, in memory of old times. The only musical accompaniment to the swinging of the poi-balls is the song of the leader of the dancers, sometimes soft and melodious, sometimes wild and high, but always truly Maori, not as with many other Maori communities a foreign air Maorified. Ancient chants, canoe-paddling time songs, and historical poems are sung to the poi-action.

The old musical instruments of the Maori, such as the various kinds of flutes, and the pakuru, a short stick held between the teeth and tapped with another stick, have long been discarded. The guitar, the ukulele, and piano are all exceedingy popular, and English and American tunes have supplemented most of the true Maori rangi or airs. The Maori is a music-loving race, with a keen sense of timc and rhythm and melody, and the singing of the various native chants is of a quality and beauty surpassed only by the wonderful music of the South Sea Island people in such places as Rarotonga, Tahiti and Samoa.

Long ago, before the ukuleles of Hawaii had been heard of, the Jew's-harp (originally Jew's-trump), roria as the Maori calls it, was the favourite instrument of music in the New Zealand village. Its rhythmic twanging was just the right accompaniment to a chant or a love ditty, and a background of roria music was exactly the thing for the poi-swinging action. The Maori could make the little harp sing; the native ear could often recognise the words of a song when the artist took the roria in hand and mouth. The original roria, in pre-pakeha times, was a short stick which when held between the teeth and twanged gave forth a plaintive sound agreeable to the ear. There is a place-name on the Northern Wairoa River which preserves a memory of the ancient prototype of the Jew's-harp. A long, slender post driven into the river bed as one of the supports of an eel-weir vibrated and hummed with the rushing of the current, and the sound it made so resembled that of the little twanging-stick that the place came to be called Tangi-te-roria.

the fitful groans and moans of Hone's trombone. By way of variety there was an occasional fife band. The most agreeable of all those bands was a party of Waikato girls who played long brass whistles and turned Moody and Sankey hymns into capital dance music.

Today, the Maori has shown that he can find a place for himself in the world of pakeha music. Opera singers, concert pianists, dance bands and vocal ensembles will become an accepted part of Maori musical life, while purely Maori cultural idiom will find its expression in action, song, haka and poi.

In games some of the old amusements have been revived, such as mati and titi-torea, the former a game played with the hands by two players seated opposite each other, the latter played with short sticks quickly thrown from one player to another. These are tests of quickness of eye and hand. Top-spinning was an old-time amusement, among old people as well as young, and there were whipping-top

The pakeha roria has quite a history in New Zealand. The story goes back to the beginnings of British colonisation; the Jew's-harp's coming was coincident with the land-bargaining of the Wakefields at Wellington and probably somewhat earlier in the North Auckland country. A venerable woman of the Hutt Valley once told me about her first Jew's-harp. It was part of the pile of goods given by "Tiraweke", otherwise Colonel Wakefield, to the chiefs and people of the Port Nicholson shores in payment for the land on which Wellington City and suburbs now stand. That was at the end of 1839, and white-haired Ngarimu reckoned she was then about fifteen years old. That was the first time she and her friends had obtained roria of their own, though they had heard all about them from other parts.

The popularity of the roria prevailed for forty years or so after that time; then other forms of music-making attracted the Maori. Brass bands came in; every large village must have its band, and the days and nights rang and banged with the brazen Wagnerisms of enthusiastic youth. It did not matter what the hour was; long before you reached the kainga you could hear the pounding of the big drum and

competitions. The older Maoris made and flew kites; it was more a pastime for the elders than for children; and these kites were large and elaborately made, often in the form of a kahu or hawk, but very much larger than that bird.

Nowadays the Maori plays with zest and proficiency every game of the pakeha. Tennis is a particularly popular recreation. The old inter-tribal rivalry which at one time developed into wars now takes the form of friendly tourna-ments with a tennis racquet. The native New Zealander is a famous footballer; there are many girls' hockey clubs, and several of the best golfers in New Zealand are Maoris. In every branch of sport, from the playing-fields to horse-racing, the Maori engages with thorough-going zest. The first Maori woman has competed at Wimbledon; many young persons take an active part in basketball and softball, while others have made their mark in woodchopping.

INDEX

In order to simplify this index, the term "Maori" to qualify various entries has in most cases been omitted; thus "language" refers to the Maori language, and so on. Names beginning with "Te" will be found entered under the initial letter of the second element of the name.